The Renegotiation of Your Retirement

THE 5 ESSENTIAL NEGOTIATIONS TO A RETIREMENT WITHOUT COMPROMISE

Frank A. Leyes, ChFC®

ISBN: 978-1791681999

Frank A. Leyes

2840 Electric Rd. St. 205-A
Roanoke, VA 24018
(540) 986-2686

Because of the dynamic nature of the Internet, web addresses or links contained in this book may have been changed since publication and may no longer be valid.

This publication contains the opinions and ideas of its author and is designed to provide useful advice in regard to the subject matter covered. The author and publisher are not engaged in rendering legal, accounting, or other professional services in this publication. This publication is not intended to provide a basis for action in particular circumstances without consideration by a competent professional. The author and publisher expressly disclaim any responsibility for any liability, loss, or risk, personal or otherwise, which is incurred as a consequence, directly or indirectly, of the use and application of any of the contents of this book.

Securities and advisory services offered through Commonwealth Financial Network®, Member FINRA/SIPC, a Registered Investment Adviser.

* The Way of Wealth, Amazon, 8/27/13, #1 in Money Management and Retirement Planning. Amazon Best Seller rankings were calculated hourly based on number of copies sold on 8/27/13 in a chosen subcategory compared to similar books in the same subcategory. Subcategories were self-selected and some subcategories contained more books than others. Recent sales were weighted more heavily than past sales. A ranking within a subcategory is not representative of total sales or placement within Amazon's overall sales list.

* The Renegotiation of Your Retirement, Amazon, 2/28/19, #1 in Private Equity, Interest, Financial Risk Management, Health Insurance, Life Insurance, Mutual Funds, Portfolio Management, Investments, Insurance, and Real Estate. Amazon Best Seller rankings were calculated hourly based on number of copies sold on 2/28/19 in a chosen subcategory compared to similar books in the same subcategory. Subcategories were self-selected and some subcategories contained more books than others. Recent sales were weighted more heavily than past sales. A ranking within a subcategory is not representative of total sales or placement within Amazon's overall sales list.

Acknowledgements

Nothing worthwhile is created without the assistance of others. We all stand on the shoulders of giants!

I would like to thank the exceptional advisors in my Advisor Mastery Group for their support in the development of this project. Their trust and input have been invaluable, and I am forever grateful to rub shoulders with the best in the industry.

I would also like to acknowledge the following:

The team at Ignite Press for their tireless work: Publishing Coordinator Malia Sexton for her patience and attention to all the moving parts, Editor Samantha Maxwell for her knowledge and attention to detail, and Everett O'Keefe for his expertise and perspective in the development and launch of this book.

To my clients for their trust,
To my family for their love,
To my God for His redemption.

Dedication

This work is dedicated to those individuals I am honored to call my peers and my friends. They help clients prepare for the changing seasons of life. They are accountable for their work. Their advice during one decade of life earns the trust of the next. They make no false promises or lofty claims. They simply do the work of planting seeds in one season and the harvesting of the next. Saving money is not glamorous. Living within one's means may not receive a lot of attention. Serving the quest of preparing for the investments known as college, starting a business, or retirement won't make the front page of any financial publication.

This work is also dedicated to my family. You put up with my grumpy moods while I strive to balance family with the stewardship of my clients' resources and the calling to share this message. Late nights, early mornings, migraines, missed movie nights, etc. were a part of the sacrifice you made for this project. The stewardship of the future is a responsibility that rightly weighs heavily on the shoulders of those of us who accept it. For every financial professional that steps into that calling, there is a family making supportive sacrifices along the way. To Jen, Nora, Isaiah, and Daniel, I love you unconditionally. I hope this work makes you proud and is worthy of the sacrifice you made to make it happen.

This entire book is based on a fundamental premise: the only path to freedom is traveled through personal responsibility. It is also dedicated to those professional advisors who accompany these individuals along the journey. This work is written with an underlying goal: good stewardship of our financial resources creates the freedom to focus on the things in life that are much more important than money. We refer to this as your "true wealth."

Table of Contents

Preface

I started my career in financial services shortly after I had a successful junior golf career and the privilege of playing for Notre Dame. It was early in my career that I found myself calling on people that I had come to know growing up around the golf course. Simply put, I was curious how some of these family acquaintances might perceive me as a fledgling financial professional.

"Greg" was in his early 50s and had been extremely successful in business. He was about to "retire" to his new home on a golf course community in the South. I wasn't actually sure why he had agreed to meet with me, but he graciously accepted my invitation. Not long into our discussion, he leaned back in his chair and put his arms behind his head. I was shocked to see a gaping hole under the left armpit of his sport coat. How could this incredibly successful and wealthy individual be wearing a jacket with a massive hole in it?

"The sooner one decides 'how much is enough,' the sooner one will be free."

In the course of our conversation, he shared something with me that has stayed with me for decades: "The sooner one decides 'how much is enough,' the sooner one will be free." Please let the wisdom of that statement sink in. I was 22 or 23 years old at the time, yet this is one of the most profound beliefs about wealth and perspective in life I have ever heard.

Throughout my career, I have witnessed the financial downfall of individuals who never came to grips with their answer to the question: "How much is enough?" Some people spend through significant incomes, windfalls, inheritances, and even lottery winnings trying to search for their answer to this question. According to the guiding philosophy of Og Mandino regarding life and wealth, "True security in life comes not from the things we have as much as from the things we choose to do without." Ironically, until one comes to terms with their own values and understanding of what money can and cannot do, they are in a prison of their own making.

The reason this "how much is enough" question may be so difficult to answer is because people do not merely want to survive. Rather, they want to thrive in the season of life known as retirement. My goal is to simplify the complexities of planning for this season of life so people can have confidence in making their transition.

But the realities of retirement are changing dramatically. The purpose of this work is to bring awareness to those changes as a prerequisite for successfully negotiating them. If this book helps you to do so, then I will have achieved my goal. Let's get started!

Introduction

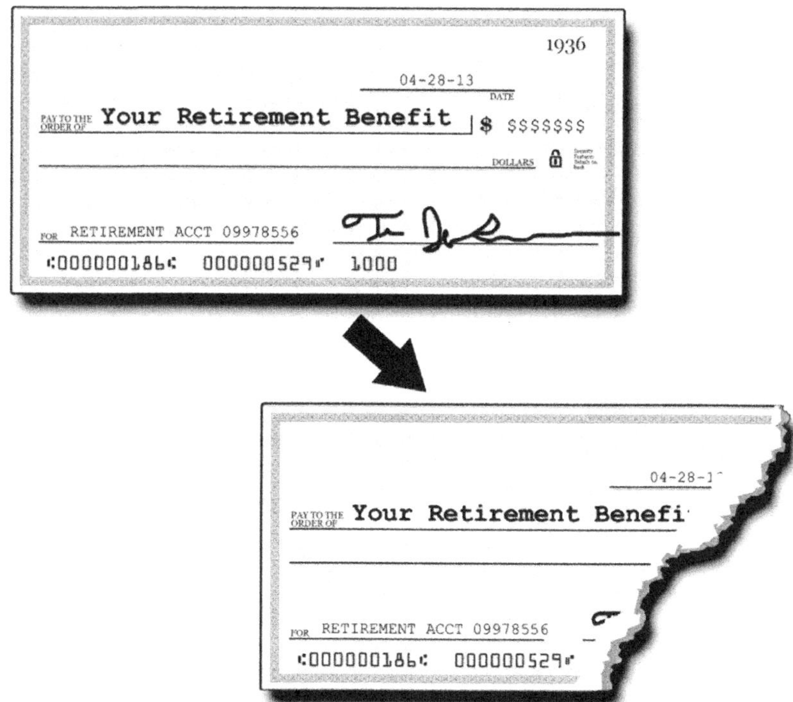

Renegotiate · *verb* · **re·ne·go·ti·ate**: To change assumptions, conditions, outcomes, or agreed-upon terms.

Imagine playing a game of Monopoly. You are halfway through the game, and suddenly… everything changes. The values of the properties you own are suddenly reduced. The prices for the properties you wish to purchase double. And even the board itself changes; it takes longer to pass "GO" than it used to. Now what?

In a very real sense, the game of retirement is going through its own transformation. Changes in health care and longevity mean we are living longer than ever. Inflation means things cost more than ever. Changes in the cost of health care mean a dollar is not going as far as it used to. And when the Federal Government steps in to "stimulate" the economy, it gets even worse.

Two-thirds of our economy is driven by consumer spending. As spending is stimulated, saving is penalized. As if these changes were not enough, look at the front page of your Social Security statement. It displays the year (rapidly approaching) when the current system will not be able to support itself. By 2033, the system will only be able to pay an estimated 75% of promised benefits. And to add even more insult to injury, the pension system is in worse condition. The number of pensions that will need bailouts from the Pension Benefit Guaranty Corporation would make Social Security look good!

> Without changes, in 2033 the Social Security Trust Fund will be able to pay only about 75 cents for each dollar of scheduled benefits.* We need to resolve these issues soon to make sure Social Security continues to provide a foundation of protection for future generations.
>
> **Social Security on the Net...**
> Visit ***www.socialsecurity.gov*** on the Internet to learn more about Social Security. You can read publications, including *When To Start Receiving Retirement Benefits*; use our Retirement Estimator to obtain immediate and personalized estimates of future benefits; and when you're ready to apply for benefits, use our improved online application—It's so easy!
>
> Michael J. Astrue
> Commissioner
>
> * These estimates are based on the intermediate assumptions from the Social Security Trustees' Annual Report to the Congress.

Source: Social Security Administration

In case you are wondering just how prepared most of us are for a retirement season that can last decades, consider the following reality check:

- The average Baby Boomer has $163,577 saved for retirement (Economic Policy Institute).
- 41% of Baby Boomers have no retirement savings at all.
- The average Social Security benefit is $1,360 per month.
- One in four 65-year olds are likely to live past age 90.
- Health care expenses in retirement are outpacing increases in Social Security benefits.
- Student loan debt now exceeds $1.5 trillion and is impacting every age group.

Maybe the Great Recession forced you into a lower-paying job right around the time you should have been hitting your peak earning stride. Or perhaps you were a victim of "The Lost Decade," in which stocks went virtually nowhere for nearly 10 years, causing your investment portfolio to take a hit. It's also a possibility that the government's quest to stimulate the economy, which drove interest rates to nearly 0%, might have reduced your earnings on CDs, money markets, and other safe investments. Or maybe the amount of time your parents spent in a nursing home cost them the inheritance they hoped to pass on to you. Even providing a decent college education for your children may have cost you far more than you had planned. Or maybe you have recently discovered that the relic pension plan you have been counting on is woefully underfunded. (Some estimate the national level of underfunded pensions to be between $5 to $8 *trillion*, or about $52,000 per household.) If you have been beset by any of these challenges, you understand the current, gut-wrenching reality of retirement. If you have yet to experience any of these, be assured that these and more challenges await.

The landscape of retirement is changing. Assumptions we once took for granted are no longer true. Markets are changing while your investments may not have earned what you anticipated. Longevity is increasing as you prepare for a retirement that is much longer than you imagined (in part because of all those supplements you took and the decision to quit smoking). With entitlement benefits potentially crushed under a demographic nightmare and a host of promises made by others (Social Security, pension plans, Medicare, etc.) that they are now fiscally incapable of keeping, this is no longer the retirement your grandparents or even your parents experienced, nor will it be the retirement you thought you were entitled to.

So what do we do with this changing landscape of what was once known as "retirement"? Do you rethink your decision to retire in the first place? Do you go into an austerity plan in the early years of retirement when most others seek to derive maximum enjoyment from health and vitality? What do you do with the lifecycle fund that may have you invested in conservative holdings now that you are on the verge of retirement? Perhaps you allowed your kids to live with you when they couldn't get jobs right out of college because it seemed like a good idea at the time. Will they feel the same way about allowing you to live with them when you make the really poor choice of outliving your retirement?

The goal of this work is to spell out how the landscape has already changed and will continue to do so. Then, we will address the steps needed to negotiate on behalf of yourself and the future you desire. If you take nothing else away from this book, please take this idea: You will experience the retirement you have negotiated. You negotiate through the well-informed and forward-thinking actions you take at each step along the journey. You don't negotiate based on the promises made by others... That merely leads to dependence. Retirement isn't a number. Retirement isn't a line. It isn't merely the end of your work career. Ken Dychtwald, gerontologist and author of *Age Wave: How the Most Important Trend of Our Time Will Change Your Future* describes retirement as our "third age." Retirement is a season of life that you define and cultivate through navigating the maze of truth and personal responsibility along the way. You will experience the exact retirement you have negotiated. Period. In this book, I will show you the way.

Welcome to the *Renegotiation of Your Retirement*. It's time we negotiate your future together!

Chapter One

The Longevity Renegotiation

Could This Be the Face of Your Retirement?

This woman's name is Jeanne Calment, and she was born in 1875. In 1965, when Jeanne was 90 years old, a 47-year-old attorney named Andre Raffray approached Jeanne with a proposition: He wanted to buy the only asset in Jeanne's name—the apartment she lived in. While Jeanne could not sell the apartment outright to Andre since she needed a place to live, she did agree to sell him the apartment on a contingency. Andre would pay Jeanne $500 per month for the rest of her life, and Andre would own the apartment upon Jeanne's death.

While this may seem like a shrewd deal for the 40-something attorney who was clearly attempting to take advantage of 90-year-old Jeanne, a twist of fate occurred. 30 years after their agreement, Andre died. You read that correctly, Andre died before Jeanne did. Jeanne would go on to live for several more years after that, eventually going into the record books as the longest-living person at the time. Jeanne turned her only asset into an income she couldn't outlive, while Andre paid approximately $180,000 for an asset he was never able to enjoy.

Or picture a scenario where you have six months until retirement. You're getting your ducks in a row, which includes a complete physical exam while you are still covered by your employer's health plan. After an exhaustive battery of tests, your doctor walks into the room with a grim look on her face.

"I'm afraid I have bad news to share with you. Based on extensive testing, including a new state-of-the-art DNA and longevity protocol, everything projects that you are likely to live to age 95." You may be asking yourself why this could be considered bad news until you reflect on the 46-page retirement plan constructed by your financial professional or robo-advisor. All of the assumptions were based on a life expectancy of 82. Now, you have to figure out how to fund an additional 13 years of retirement. Longevity is both a blessing and a challenge. What is your plan?

Actuaries are among the most powerful and influential voices inside of the insurance industry. Their work underlies some of the most far-reaching and critical strategies for managing risk among these financial giants. Their research determines the pricing upon which products are designed. Their work helps craft the products that the marketing department promotes and the underwriting department manages—the products that investment portfolios are all designed to support. Don't let the stereotype of coke bottle glasses and geeks in cubicles distract you from the essential message echoing from this group. These actuaries are planning for a reality that you and I also need to acknowledge: Longevity is changing the game.

The most recent innovations in insurance products have an underlying assumption you must recognize. Before an insurance company can assume a risk, it must quantify that risk. The starting point for that evaluation is longevity. Believe it or not, many of these insurance products are now designed to work around policyholders that live to age 105! You read that right: 105! If the insurance companies are renegotiating around the vastly changing landscape of longevity, so must you.

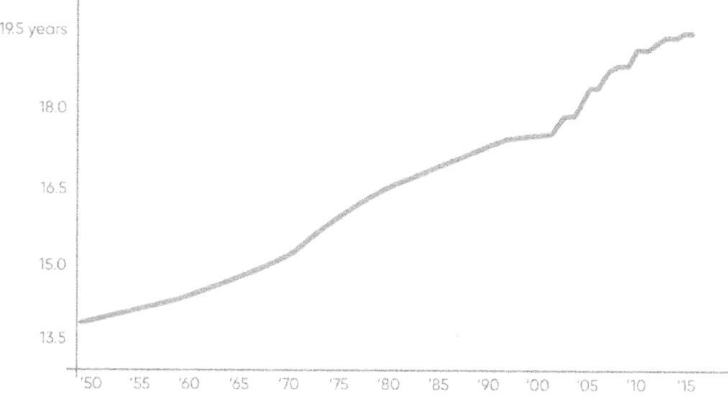

Data source: Voya Financial

"If I would have known I was going to live this long, I would have taken better care of myself."

—Mickey Mantle

Source: Life Images

The Pill and the Protocol

Your DNA has been tested. Stem cells have been collected to replenish or rejuvenate other damaged cells or casualties of the aging process. Specific nutrition and supplementation and exercise regimens have been tailored to your exact, unique body. Range-of-motion testing isolates areas that are prone to restriction or injury. Cutting-edge strength training helps you hone in on the areas that can keep you strong, flexible, and well-balanced for decades to come.

Genetic testing is already starting to recognize some of the hereditary issues we are all born with. "I was just born this way" is no longer an excuse. "Blame it on Mom and Dad" gives way to a story of empowerment, choice, and personal responsibility. A battery of tests that may have seemed like science fiction not that long ago are now both affordable and practical. You are now presented with a path to health and vitality that leverages every breakthrough in health, wellness, nutrition, nanotechnology, and medical science. You are presented with a pill (or a protocol) that is likely to add 20% to your life expectancy. Will you take it?

Years and decades of planning, saving, eliminating debt, and projecting needed funds to retire have just been... blown up. Breakthroughs in every area mentioned above are imposing the need to reimagine, reinvent, and redesign the season of life known as retirement. Before you answer the question as to whether you will take the longevity pill, there is a consequence to consider. Would you still take the pill if you knew it would "cost" 20% of your life savings?

The price of this "longevity pill" is not solely in what it may cost to take it. Rather, the price is reflected in issues with funding the additional years of life it may help you achieve.

A breakthrough in one area of life has a potential consequence in another. The actuaries inside the cubicles of insurance companies have been secretly planning for this for years. As insurance policies are redesigned for the era of longevity, the insurance companies are now planning to reserve for a lifespan up to 120 years. If their solvency depends upon adequately planning and preparing for this eventuality, we are left with no choice but to do the same.

"One of the conclusions we came to, early on,
was that the traditional notion of retiring in your early 60s
was a bad idea... 70 is the new 65."

—Steve Vernon, scholar, Stanford Center on Longevity

LIFE EXPECTANCY

	65-year old man	65-year old woman	65-year old couple*
50% chance	**87 years**	**90 years**	**94 years**
25% chance	**92 years**	**96 years**	**98 years**

*At least one surviving individual.
Source: Society of Actuaries RP-2014 Mortality Table projected with Mortality Improvement Scale MP-2014 as of 2015. For illustrative purposes.

Are you prepared to spend the next 35 years in retirement? When we consider that this also happens to be the point in life where your greatest health care expenses occur, are you truly ready? According to data from HealthView Services, an average, healthy 65-year-old couple who lives two years beyond their projected life expectancy will incur an additional $91,496 in total retirement health care costs (future value).

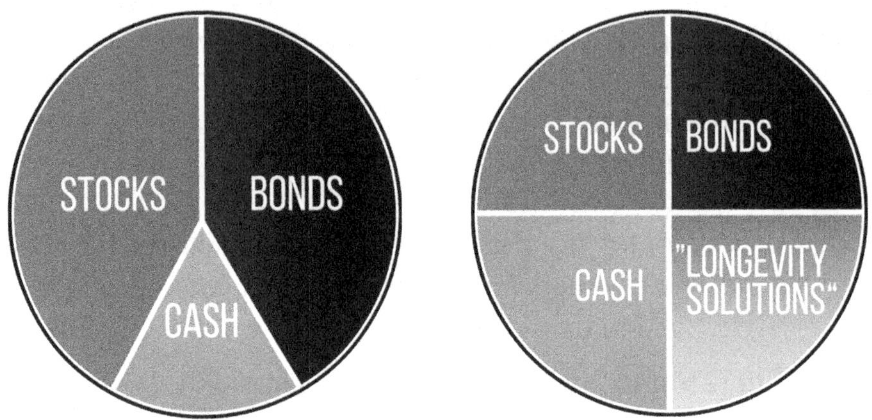

The Long-Term Care Discussion

This issue may be the elephant in the room of retirement planning. Currently, there are nearly 50 million Americans age 65 or older according to the census. But by 2060, this number is projected to grow to 98.2 million. That is nearly 100% growth in the number of people age 65 or older in just over 40 years! What's more, 70% of individuals who reach age 65 will need long-term care at some point in their lives (Source: "The Basics" at LongTermCare.gov).

Here are some more challenging numbers for you:

- The *median* cost of a private room in a long-term care facility in 2018 is $8,121 per month.
- The median cost of a semi-private room is $7,148 per month. That's $85,776 a year!

- The average stay is 2.6 years for women and 2.3 years for men. This equals an average cost (in a semi-private room) of $223,017 for women and $197,284 for men.
- Almost half of the people living in nursing homes are age 85 or older.

10 to 15 years ago, it was not uncommon for individuals to negotiate this risk by purchasing long-term care insurance policies. Today, those options are substantially different. The extended period of artificially low interest rates limited what insurance companies were able to earn on their reserves for future claims. Claims on long-term care policies were more frequent than insurance companies had anticipated and for longer stays than they anticipated as well. In addition, the cost of long-term care facilities outpaced their earlier projections. In short, the insurance companies projected a reasonable profit from long-term care policies but lost a great deal of money instead. As a result, a number of insurance companies (Metlife, TIAA-CREF, CIGNA, Genworth) have left the long-term care industry completely. Other companies have imposed significant premium increases to those maintaining these policies. For the insurance companies continuing to offer long-term care policies, the premiums today are substantially higher than in the earlier generations of policies. These changes have paved the way for a new generation of solutions for the long-term care risk. Some of these newer offerings are asset-based solutions, policies with long-term care benefits tied to a savings and/or death benefit. While they are dramatically different than the traditional long-term care policies, they are an increasingly popular strategy for addressing this issue.

How Insurance Really Works

While it is a complex industry, insurance companies make money through a relatively straightforward process. In exchange for taking on a risk (auto accident, house fire, death), they collect money (in the form of premiums) from you. A portion of this money is then invested in a wide variety of investments, some of which may also have preferential tax treatment. Over time, the insurance company may earn returns from these investments. Even if the company ultimately pays you the entire premium that you have paid, the company's goal is to have earned enough money in the interim so that the insurance policy is still profitable. In addition, insurance companies dilute their risk among multiple policies. Using extremely thorough research and a careful analysis of actuarial tables, insurance companies can determine their risk of loss for any given policy and set rates that are likely to allow the company to cover any potential claims while still producing a profit for the company. When this practice is duplicated across thousands (or hundreds of thousands) of policies, the insurance company can usually withstand even catastrophic losses from a few claims.

Problems arise, however, when the reality of actual claims, expenses, and yields on reserves differ from what was assumed when the policy was initially priced. If the company prices a specific insurance product based upon incorrect assumptions, the company can lose a substantial amount of money rather than make a profit. This can also occur if the insurance company is forced to pay too many large claims. If these situations occur enough, the insurance company will be forced to either increase the price of the product, "water down" the product so it provides fewer benefits, or stop offering the product entirely.

We have seen this over and over again. The most obvious example can be seen following major natural disasters. In the 20 years before Hurricane Katrina struck New Orleans, insurance companies in Louisiana collected approximately $8 billion in premiums. After paying premiums before Katrina, they had earned about $1 billion in profits from this. But when Katrina hit in 2005, homeowners' insurance claims topped $8 billion. In other words, the insurance companies paid approximately $16 billion ($8 billion in the 20 years before 2005 and $8 billion in the year of Katrina). Experts determined that it would take more than a century to recoup these losses… unless changes were made.

So changes were made! Some insurance companies decided to stop selling homeowners insurance in Louisiana. Those who continued to sell insurance chose to increase their rates and/or further limit their coverage (water down their product). As a result, homeowners insurance in Louisiana is expensive! According to Insurance Hunter, "Ever since Hurricane Katrina, the state regularly ranks as one of the most expensive for homeowners insurance in the U.S., alongside areas like Florida and Texas, two other states which are often in the path of hurricanes" (Source: https://www.insurancehunter.ca/blog/impact-hurricane-katrina-insurance-industry).

Insurance companies providing long-term care have experienced their own Katrina. But rather than a storm of sudden devastation, they have experienced a perfect storm of a widening gap between assumptions and experience. The historically low interest rates we have experienced, especially since 2009, have resulted in lower-than-anticipated earnings on reserves for some insurance companies offering long-term care policies. The research and actuarial data they used to set the prices of their LTC policies caused them to overestimate the amount of money they would make through premiums. Simply put, these companies had no way of knowing that interest rates (and, therefore, the returns on their investments) would drop so low and stay so low for so long. In addition to interest rates staying lower than expected, claims have been higher than expected, and the cost of care and facilities has been growing at a rate higher than projected. As a result, they put too low a price tag on their long-term care policies. While this resulted in a great bargain for those who bought LTC policies in the 90s, it ultimately caused the insurance companies to lose a great deal of money. Therefore, they had to do what insurance companies did following Katrina. Some companies removed themselves from the market entirely, discontinuing the sale of LTC policies completely. Those that remained increased their prices and tightened up on the benefits of these policies. As such, the LTC insurance options available to you are quite different than they were 20 years ago.

Even though insurance companies can become easy targets during political seasons, there is a fundamental point I would like to make. If insurance companies cannot adequately underwrite and price for a risk and cannot administer claims appropriately, they cannot be profitable. If you and I are depending on an insurance company to make good in the future on promises they make yesterday and today, we want them to be profitable.

Long-Term Care Solutions

The solutions to the long-term care issue invariably fall into one of three categories:

1. The government solution

Medicare currently pays for a fraction of long-term care expenses (only skilled care, immediately following a hospital stay, and for a very limited number of days). The other government solution is at the state level and is administered through Medicaid. Unfortunately, one needs to be "impoverished" before the states will cover the cost of care. Individual states will define "impoverished" in their own ways. And the Medicaid program will determine where care is to be received.

2. The insurance solution
   Whether you are looking at a traditional long-term care insurance policy or a newer hybrid, asset-based solution, the cost for insurance is significant.
3. Self insurance
   If you choose not to purchase insurance, you have by default chosen the path of "self insurance." You have, in effect, decided that you will personally cover all expenses as they occur. Remember this: an "average" stay of 2.3 years at a semi-private room rate of $7,148 comes to $197,284. These are 2018 statistics. Depending on when you need care, this number is likely to be substantially (and perhaps *dramatically*) higher.

The Frailty Negotiation and the Continuing Care Retirement Community

You read that correctly: the frailty negotiation. While updating my research on long-term care, a new and growing condition has surfaced in retirement planning research. To qualify for most long-term care policies, one must demonstrate an inability to complete two or more activities of daily living.

Activities of Daily Living

Activities of Daily Living (or ADLs) is a catch-all phrase for the tasks we do when we are fully independent and that we may no longer be able to do when our health is compromised. This potential list can include tasks like mowing your yard, painting your home, cleaning out your gutters, snow removal, and other physically demanding activities. But it can also include basic tasks such as paying your own bills and keeping your financial world organized and secure (especially in today's era of cybercrime and other well-documented attempts to defraud seniors).

Activities of Daily Living:

- Bathing:
    - Getting into a tub or shower
    - Getting out of a tub or shower
    - Washing your body in a tub, shower, or by sponge bath
    - Washing your hair in a tub, shower, or sink
- Dressing:
    - Putting on any necessary item of clothing (including undergarments) and any necessary braces, fasteners, or artificial limbs
    - Taking off any necessary item of clothing (including undergarments) and any necessary braces, fasteners, or artificial limbs

Transferring:

- Getting into a bed, chair, or wheelchair
- Getting out of a bed, chair, or wheelchair

Toileting:

- Getting to and from the toilet
- Getting on and off the toilet
- Performing associated personal hygiene

Continence:

- Maintaining control of bowel and bladder function
- Performing associated personal hygiene (including caring for catheter or colostomy bag)

Eating:

- Feeding yourself by getting food into your mouth from a container (such as a plate or cup), including the use of utensils when appropriate (such as a spoon or fork)
- When unable to feed yourself from a container, feeding yourself by a feeding tube or intravenously

The inability to perform these ADLs is described as "frailty." While it may be impossible to know when frailty will occur and, therefore, difficult to perfectly plan for it, there are a few common-sense steps that can help address this proactively:

- Build a buffer into your budget that might include additional funds to pay someone to mow your yard, shovel snow, etc.
- Decide in advance if you would like to have someone on call for backup as it relates to overseeing your finances (this can include everything from providing them with duplicate statements or online access to view your accounts).
- Agree to a 24-hour rule relative to any solicitation you receive over the phone or online. This will help protect you against those who are opportunistic and attempting to take advantage of you. Discuss the solicitation with a trusted friend, advisor, or family member before acting on it. Always remember that if an offer sounds too good to be true, it probably is.

In consideration of frailty and possible long-term care issues, some are drawn to the concept of living in continuing care retirement communities. These communities allow someone to age in place. While those living in these communities remain independent, they have the option for increased care if or when it is needed, ultimately giving the residents of these communities some peace of mind in their long-term care decisions.

These communities can be expensive to join at the outset. In return for this significant investment, they do allow for the progression of care and life management as it is needed. There is one significant requirement to keep in mind when considering this type of living arrangement. One must be healthy and independent in order to move into the community.

I was having a conversation with a client who was preparing to relocate to a new town to live closer to children and grandchildren. A CCRC was one of the options she was exploring. When the time came for a decision on where to live, she ruled out the CCRC. Her comments were, "I'm simply not ready for that type of a living situation yet" (she valued her independence greatly). "I understand," I replied. "But we need to keep in mind that the specific issue that could arise that would make you 'ready' (some diminished capacity) could be the same issue they use to reject your application."

While longevity is changing the game, longevity itself is both a blessing and a challenge: You cannot protect yourself from it, so it is essential that you provide for it! Perhaps it's time to begin renegotiating your retirement.

Want to know your life expectancy?
Visit https://www.livingto100.com/

Acknowledging that personal responsibility is
the only path to freedom
We make informed decisions
Taking action with the resources we have
Adjusting course along the way
Focusing only on what we can control
Until the future you envision in the present
Becomes the reality that you experience.

Chapter 2

The Entitlements Renegotiation

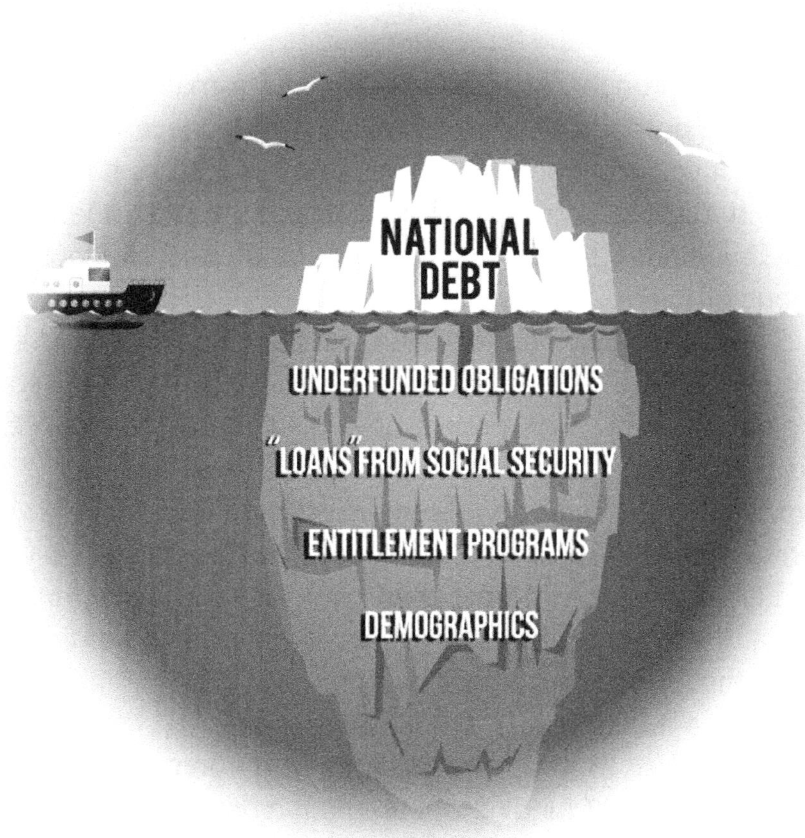

Blame It on Ida!

Blame it on Ida! In 1940, the first Social Security payment was distributed to Ida Mae Fuller. Her check (#00000001) was for the amount of $22.54. Over the course of Ida Mae's retirement years, she received a total of $22,888.92. This isn't a bad "return" given the fact that she only paid $24.75 into the system! If you are anticipating a similar "return," you may want to continue reading and adjust your expectations accordingly.

The Changing Demographics of Social Security

Let's approach retirement in terms of a math problem: 15 people are on one side of a room. 12 people leave. How many remain? If you are wondering if it's a trick question, it isn't. The trick is not in the simplicity of this question. Rather, the trick is in the avoidance techniques some have utilized to ignore the obvious problem.

Even as recently as the 1950s, we have had 15 workers for each retiree. Allow me to illustrate the challenge of the system. Let's say the original 15 people have a job to do. Their job is to fund the retirement of the one person on the other side of the room. That single person's retirement will come to $234,432. This figure assumes the average Social Security benefit of a 66-year-old ($1,221 per month) multiplied over their life expectancy of age 82. If we divide the cost of this single person's retirement among the 15 people originally in the room, we split the cost of the retirement benefit to $15,629 per person.

Now, back to the exodus from the room... Instead of dividing the cost of funding a retirement among 15 people, let's recalculate the cost to only three people covering the same cost.

$234,432/3 = $78,144. We just raised the cost from $15,629 per person to $78,144 per person! Welcome to the changing demographics of the Social Security system. When the system began, there were 41 workers retirees for each benefit recipient (and that recipient was not expected to live very long once retired!). Now, we are down to three.

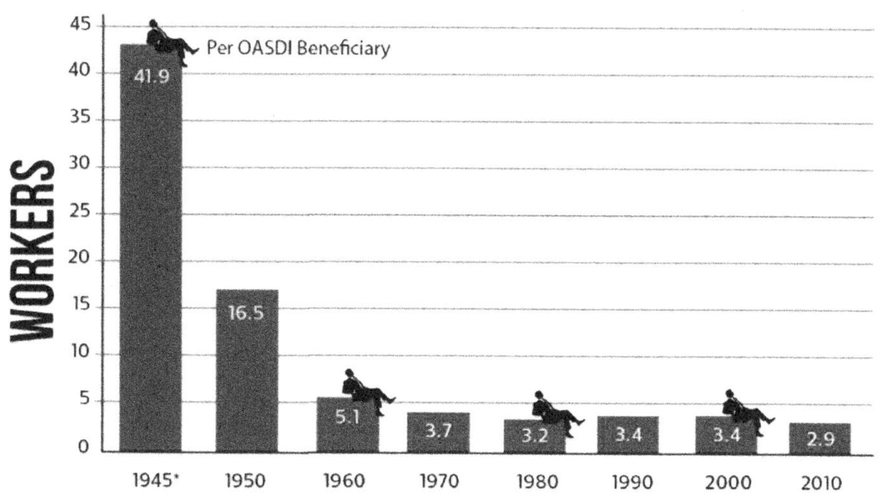

Source: 2012 OASDI Trustee Report, Table IV.B2. www.ssa.gov, accessed May 21, 2012.
Data note: The Trustee Report provides data from 1945 and onward. Prior estimates are unavailable.
Produced by Veronique de Rugy Mercatus Center at George Mason University.

Social Security was Never Designed for This

The system we call Social Security was designed to be a safety net: a minimum amount of assistance to help individuals have a financial baseline for life in retirement, in the event of disability, or as a surviving spouse or child. It was never intended to be a primary source of income for retirees. Yet it has become just that. And the system has major problems:

- When Social Security was first enacted on August 14th, 1935 as part of the New Deal, there were 40 workers for each retiree. Today, there are three.
- The Social Security "Trust Fund" has become merely another source of excessive government spending.

Designed to help provide for the Baby Boomers, the fund has been systematically raided by our government. It is against the law for an employer to borrow money from its employees' retirement funds. Why is it okay for the federal government? In order to pay back what it owes to Social Security recipients, the government must now either increase taxes (likely) or reduce benefits (politically unpopular).

The last time the system was comprehensively reviewed and revised was the back in 1983, through the Greenspan Commission. As a result of this commission, payroll taxes increased, and the full retirement age was moved back. If we ever decide to address this problem again, expect more of the same. The longer we delay addressing the problem, the more severe the solution will need to be. This principle is the same whether we are speaking of the Social Security system or an individual preparing for retirement. Time is the enemy of the procrastinator and the ally of the negotiator.

Time is the enemy of the procrastinator
and the ally of the negotiator.

How do you negotiate with this underfunded entitlement? Vote responsibly for individuals willing to make difficult choices to reconnect the "security" with the "social." We often hear government leaders state that they will never reduce benefits for this all-important controversial issue. The problem is that there is no way to address the underlying math problem of exploding entitlement budgets without cuts. Taxes are going to go up. The age for eligibility for benefits will be moved back. And there may be an introduction to the controversial concept of "means testing." This idea is that benefits are reduced for those who earn incomes above a certain threshold. There is simply no way to manage our exploding debt and budgets without changes to entitlement programs. While people are quick to label those who engage this challenging issue as "political", this generalization ignores the fundamental nature of the challenge. The exploding deficits associated with our entitlement problems is essentially a math problem that must be addressed in an open and constructive dialog. Personally, I prefer to vote for individuals willing to have this honest discussion. But until that discussion occurs, be prepared to fund the foundation of your own retirement without dependence on an underfunded future promise. Personal responsibility remains the only path to freedom.

There is one thing you cannot afford in retirement: dependence upon social security. There is a math related to the state of dependence, and it's not a pretty sight. Lifestyle decisions, spending decisions, health care decisions, family decisions, and financial decisions will all be based on a system over which we have no control.

According to the 2018 Trustees Report, for the first time since 1982, the Social Security system will pay out more in benefits than it takes in. As though this news isn't bad enough, it goes on to project that *this status will continue for the next*

75 years! Unless Congress acts, by the year 2033, the system will only be able to pay 75% of currently projected benefits. The combination of an aging population, increases in life expectancies, and lower birth rates are all contributing factors. For every year we delay to address the problem, the cost of the solution increases dramatically.

Permit me to mention the blatantly obvious. Revising the Social Security system is not a politically popular issue. In fact, it is often referred to as the "third rail." This is how the keeper of all knowledge, Wikipedia, describes the third rail:

"The **third rail** of a nation's politics is a metaphor for any issue so controversial that it is 'charged' and 'untouchable' to the extent that any politician or public official who dares to broach the subject will invariably suffer politically."

If you had to vote on one or more of the following adjustments to the current system, which would you choose?

Increased payroll taxes?

Delayed age of qualification for benefits?

Increased taxation of social security benefits?

"Means testing" (reducing benefits for those who have more than an arbitrarily selected number of assets or amount of income)?

The list above represents factors that were adjusted the last time a meaningful revision to the Social Security system occurred, which was the Greenspan Commission in 1983. Let's take a moment to consider the shift in demographics that have occurred since that time.

Approximately 10,000 Baby Boomers are retiring per day. The largest generation in history is cascading into retirement. In the past, we were able to delay taking our medicine regarding the underfunded promises of Social Security *because of demographics.* With the sheer numbers of Baby Boomers entering their peak earning years, we were able to phase in the adjustments needed to keep the system solvent. What do we do now that the largest generation in history is in its retirement season? The size of the generation behind us is not large enough for us to adopt another phased-in approach to solving the problem over time.

The greatest challenge with entitlement programs may be the level to which they are impacted by demographics. In a system that was initially designed with 43 workers per retiree, the mathematical reality of today's demographics of three workers per retiree is challenging all by itself. This problem is magnified by the fact that entitlement programs are considered untouchable in today's political climate. AARP (American Association of Retired Persons) is the largest non-profit in the country. It is a significant force to be reckoned with as it relates to the demographic of individuals over age 50. Any politician willing to address the extent to which entitlement programs are underfunded also faces the challenge of taking on this coalition. Perhaps two quotes will help to frame the challenge and what is riding on our long-term ability to fund our promises:

"A democracy cannot exist as a permanent form of government.
It can only exist until the voters discover that they can vote themselves money from the public treasury."

—Sir Alexander Fraser Tytler,
The Decline and Fall of the Athenian Republic

"Dr. Franklin, what have you given us?"
"Madam, we have given you a Republic, if you can keep it."

—Benjamin Franklin

In a fascinating interview, former President George W. Bush revealed that he felt the greatest failure of his presidency was his failure to address the problems with Social Security. According to his interview in *The Guardian* (June 4, 2010), Bush said that "his greatest disappointment as President was failing to push through Social Security reform. Bush said that the GOP leadership balked at the proposal, saying that it would cost them votes." Part of his proposed solution to the problems facing Social Security was to allow the option for individuals to have control over and privately invest in a portion of the fund. Mr. Bush's presidency ended in 2009. There has been no meaningful discussion on how to address the problem since.

Albert Einstein was quoted as saying, "Compound interest is the eighth wonder of the world. He who understands it, earns it... He who doesn't... pays it. Compound interest is the most powerful force in the universe." Every year that we delay solving this problem will increase its cost. In the mathematics of dependence, one cannot afford to have the core of their financial equation under someone else's control. Clearly, Social Security is not going away. It has gone from being a mere safety net to a central underpinning of the retirement plans of the majority of Americans.

Your most important decision regarding Social Security is a simple yet difficult one. You cannot afford to be dependent upon it.

Secrets to Claiming the Right Social Security Strategy

You have probably received dinner invitations from firms that claim to have the secret sauce to squeeze every dollar out of your Social Security benefits. Social media and radio ads are filled with promises that may turn you into the next Ida Mae Fuller. Will you permit me to cut through all of the noise and drill down to the single incontrovertible issue that is absolutely 100% guaranteed to determine your optimum Social Security strategy? (Even that last sentence sounds like some of those free dinner invitations.) Okay, are you ready? This single strategy alone will be worth multiples of your investment in this book. I simply need to know one piece of information to deliver this promise. I need to know... when you are going to die. Seriously. If you can give me that single piece of information, I can hone in on the perfect Social Security strategy for you.

Okay, seriously, in the absence of that unknowable, there is a decision tree that we utilize to help develop your Social Security strategy. It is based on both economic and non-economic factors, such as:

- Do you intend to retire before your full retirement age (FRA)? Knowing your full retirement age is extremely important. Your benefits are discounted based on how many years prior to your FRA that you initiate benefits.
- If you plan to begin receiving benefits before your FRA, do you plan to keep working? There are significant penalties or offsets to your benefits if your earnings are above the specified threshold.
- Are there any health factors that may impact your longevity in retirement? Delaying the receipt of benefits based on a generic life expectancy model that may not reflect your health conditions could be a misguided strategy.
- Is there a parent or spouse that may need assistance with care during your retirement years?

- If you elect to receive your Social Security benefits prior to your FRA, how do you envision using the income (i.e., if the benefits could help to eliminate debts and their associated payments, this may offset the discount from taking your Social Security early)? Others may take the benefit and reinvest it into an account over which they have greater control.

The evaluation of your optimal Social Security benefits can be complicated. It is an important and irrevocable decision. Believe it or not, you can begin planning for it years ahead of time. Currently, for each year you defer the receipt of benefits beyond your earliest year of eligibility (62 at the time of this writing), the increase in the future Social Security benefit is almost 8%. One approach to allow these benefits to grow is to build up a fund that is not associated with retirement. We might refer to this as a "bridge fund." The goal of this fund might be to bridge the time frame between when you stop working and the date when you begin receiving your Social Security benefits. The time for negotiating your Social Security decision is years before you get there.

Note on Educational Events (a.k.a. "Free Dinners")

I have no problem with a financial professional who chooses to do educational events for current and prospective clients. Sometimes, a meal is involved as a way to entice people to attend. There is nothing inherently wrong with these events. However, there is a "smell test" I would encourage you to use to aid your discernment if you attend an event like this. In a recent conversation, a gentleman told me he received an invitation to a dinner seminar promising to cover the myriad of choices involved in evaluating Social Security benefit options. Just 15 minutes into the event, the subject matter changed completely. The rest of the evening was a pitch for an unrelated financial product. If you ever find yourself in a similar set of circumstances, you may wish to politely finish your meal and excuse yourself.

For over 15 years, I have had the privilege of coordinating a financial education program with one of the largest educational institutions in the country. Financial education can be a cornerstone of financial literacy and the establishment of the groundwork for solid decision-making. The decisions we sow today will shape the harvest we reap in the future.

If a financial professional is willing to misguide you at an introductory educational event (in which they advertise one topic then quickly switch to another), it may be a warning sign that warrants very close scrutiny. There is nothing wrong with a free meal or a professional using these events to educate and meet clients who may be in need of the services of a financial professional. But you should be discerning if the promise of education becomes a persuasive pitch in clever disguise.

Acknowledging that personal responsibility is
the only path to freedom
We make informed decisions
Taking action with the resources we have
Adjusting course along the way
Focusing only on what we can control
Until the future you envision in the present
Becomes the reality that you experience.

Chapter 3

The Pensions Renegotiation

No Pension, No Problem... Unless...

A promise made is a promise kept… unless it isn't. A promise is only as good as the resources behind it. Lately, promises have been broken and sold, and pension plans are going the way of the dinosaurs.

While meeting with one of my business clients, the conversation became very awkward. His company's pension plan was underfunded to the point where action had to be taken. To get back on schedule, the company had to either reduce future benefits, increase contributions to the plan, or find a way to earn greater returns on the pension fund's holdings. Whichever path the company chose, the law stated that employees needed to be informed about the health of the pension plan and the steps being taken to restore it to appropriate levels. My client looked at me and asked me to deliver that message to the employees. If ever there was a case of "don't shoot the messenger," this was it.

There are very good reasons why you should be concerned with the pension crisis even if you are not covered under a pension plan. The manner in which this crisis is addressed may give an indication as to how other underfunded promises will be handled.

De-risk

"Plan Sponsors Must De-risk Employee 401(k) Loans From Default"

-Employee Benefit Adviser Magazine 7/3/18

"Conditions Are Ripe for Employers to De-risk Their Pension Plans"

-Employee Benefit News 5/23/18

If you are not familiar with the term "de-risk," don't feel out of place. This term is one of the most recent examples of the creation a new term to put a fresh spin on an unpopular topic. The term "junk bonds" has been replaced with "high-yield bonds." The process of hiding something on one's financial statement is sometimes referred to as moving a risk or an asset "off line" or "above/below the line."

Make no mistake, there really is no such thing as "de-risking" (which, by the way, shows up 996,000 times in Google). Rather, there is a process of transferring risk from one party to another. Welcome to your "party." One perspective on the scope of the problem (even including any attempts to "de-risk") suggests that if pension funds tried to buy an annuity from an insurance company to fund these future promises, they would be short by $5 trillion! Consider the following statistics from an article in *ThinkAdvisor* entitled "Meet Your Multiemployer Pension Nightmare: Actuary to Lawmakers" by Allison Bell, published on April 19, 2018:

- The U.S. has roughly 10 million people covered in 1,400 pension plans.

- Approximately 100 of those plans are likely to fail in the next 20 years.
- The Pension Benefit Guaranty Corporation (PBGC), the agency that insures pension plans, has roughly $2.2 billion in assets. It needs roughly $67 billion just to cover obligations to participants in plans that have already failed!
- The PBGC could run out of funds around 2025.

The reason the PBGC is so vitally important is magnified by considering the fact that the typical pension plan in America is significantly underfunded. According to a recent study by Milliman Public Pension Funding, the 100 largest pension plans in the U.S. are estimated to be funded at 70.7% of their liability (June 2017). In other words, they don't have enough money to back up their promises. A similar study on state and local government pensions estimated them to be funded at 39% of future promises. Between 2009 and 2016,

- 33% of public sector employers increased employee contribution rates
- 22% changed plan design
- 17% reduced benefits
- 8% increased eligibility requirements
- 7% increased the vesting period

A Willis Towers Watson study revealed that from 1998 to 2013, the number of Fortune 500 companies offering traditional, defined benefit plans dropped 86% from 251 to 34! Brad Smith, a consultant with a Boston-based consulting firm, has said, "We expect that approximately 25% of workers with an active pension are likely to see the plan close or freeze at some point in the future."

Remember that the Pension Benefit Guaranty Corporation provides a form of insurance to help ensure the benefits that have been promised to pensioners. Some have described the Pension Benefit Guaranty Corporation as having a similar to role to FDIC (Federal Deposit Guaranty Corporation) insurance, which backs up bank deposits.

Your bank has a sort of insurance policy with the FDIC. If the bank goes out of business and is unable to return your money, all or part of your money will be provided to you by the FDIC. But what if the FDIC ran low on money and was only able to pay you pennies on the dollar? This hypothetical question may reflect the reality of the Pension Benefit Guaranty Corporation.

So, why is this your problem even though you may not be covered under a pension? The amount of funding for the scope of the problem may go far beyond the ability of the PBGC to address on its own. As the chart below illustrates, there may be a "bailout" in the making. The PBGC has no money of its own. It is funded by contributions from companies that have pension plans. If these contributions are not sufficient to keep plans solvent, the American taxpayer should watch out. We may ultimately be the final resort as these plans "de-risk." Watch carefully how this development unfolds.

You must negotiate on behalf of your own future. Pension promises may very likely be broken. Those who have negotiated on behalf of their own futures (through additional savings and investments) may be able to absorb the fallout better than those without such a measure of financial independence.

Remember, personal responsibility is the only path to freedom. Negotiate today… or compromise later.

Acknowledging that personal responsibility is
the only path to freedom
We make informed decisions
Taking action with the resources we have
Adjusting course along the way
Focusing only on what we can control
Until the future you envision in the present
Becomes the reality that you experience.

P.S. The Retirement Time Machine: Your Early Retirement Offer

It's no secret that employees closest to retirement are also the most expensive ones for employers to keep. A mature employee may be higher on the pay and benefits scale. When cost-cutting becomes a primary motivation, an employer may seek to reduce their overhead by offering an early retirement package. These packages can be complicated. Given the number of variables they often cover, they should be thoughtfully evaluated with the help of a financial professional. These decisions are usually permanent. A detailed process for evaluating these options can either leverage years of good retirement planning or diminish its impact. The following graphic entitled "5 Steps to Evaluate a Retirement Package" is designed to serve as a starting point for your evaluation of an offer that may come your way. While we have chosen to put this summary at the end of the chapter on pensions, these questions can apply to individuals with other types of retirement plans as well. Always keep in mind that the tax and legal aspects of evaluating a potential offer should be explored with a tax, accounting, or legal professional.

Step 1: Social Security Options

In regard to Social Security, there are several pieces of information you will want to have, including your full retirement age (FRA), the impact of earned income on Social Security benefits if you continue working, the discount for electing to receive Social Security before your FRA, your break-even point, and your personal health status and its possible impacts.

1. Are you aware of your what your full retirement age is? Or that is has slowly but surely been increasing since the 1950s? The following is a breakdown of FRA:

Year Born:	Full Retirement Age:
1943–1954	66
1955	66 and 2 months
1956	66 and 4 months
1957	66 and 6 months
1958	66 and 8 months
1959	66 and 10 months
1960+	67

2. Be conscious of the impact of earned income on your Social Security benefits if you continue working and elect to take Social Security prior to your full retirement age. If you earn *less than $17,640*, there is no impact, but if you earn above $17,640, you forfeit $1 in Social Security benefits for every $2 in earned income above $17,640.
3. Familiarize yourself with the discount for electing to receive Social Security *before* your full retirement age. For example (assuming 66 is FRA):

Electing Benefits at Age:	% of Full Retirement Benefit:
62	75%
63	80%
64	86.66%
65	93.33%
66	100%

4. Be knowledgeable about your break-even point, which can be defined as the point in which total cost and total revenue are “equal” or “even.” While electing

benefits before your full retirement age results in a lower benefit amount per year, it also provides you with a head start. Someone electing benefits at age 62 has a four-year head start on someone who waits until age 66. This head start can lead to a benefit advantage that can last approximately 12 years. If you collect Social Security benefits for 12 years or less, you will collect more money by starting early. However, if you end up collecting benefits for more than 12 years, you will receive higher benefits by waiting until you are at your full retirement age. This is considered your break-even point.

5. Be cognizant of your personal health status and its possible impact on your longevity.

For example, if you have excellent health and a family history of longevity, you might benefit from deferring benefits until you reach your FRA. However, if you have serious health conditions or a medical history that could limit longevity, you may receive more benefits by starting them sooner. Visit www.ssa.gov for more resources on Social Security.

Step 2: Can You Afford to Retire?

The second step is to consider whether or not you can afford to retire. To do so, it is advised that you take several factors into consideration, which includes reviewing monthly expenses, listing both “fixed” and “variable” sources of income, and paying off debt versus investing.

1. Review monthly expenses by considering budget areas that change upon retirement, like work-related expenses decreasing while travel and health care expenses increase.

2. List "fixed" sources of income like pension benefits, annuity income, and/or military or government retirement.
3. List "variable" sources of income. Conventional studies indicate that a 4% withdrawal rate is generally sustainable in retirement (although not guaranteed). In other words, $100,000 in investment/retirement value can yield $4,000 per year in income. Annuitization, or the process of exchanging a sum of money for a lifetime income payment, can deliver retirement benefits above 4%. However, you should keep the following in mind: This process involves permanently moving your money to an insurance company. When payouts are calculated, current interest rates play a significant role in the formula (i.e., interest rates hovering near 50-year lows translate into low lifetime income payments), and this strategy offers little to no inflation protection.
4. Consider whether you should pay off debt or invest. This is an individual evaluation, but some criteria to consider include stress, cash flow, and earnings of investments compared to the interest rate of your mortgage. Is the debt causing a level of emotional, spiritual, or financial stress in your life? Will paying off the debt make a greater impact on your cash flow than simply leaving the funds invested and servicing the debt?

For example, assume you have $50,000 remaining on your mortgage and a payment of $750 per month. If you had $50,000 invested instead, this could generate $2,000 per year of income at a 4% withdrawal rate. On the other hand, if you used the $50,000 to eliminate your mortgage, you may save $9,000 per year ($750 monthly mortgage payments x 12 months). However, you should keep the impact of taxes in mind. Withdrawals from a retirement account are generally taxable as ordinary income, while interest on a home mortgage is generally tax-deductible.

Lastly, you can compare the potential earnings rate on your investments (which may not be guaranteed) with the interest costs of your mortgage (often guaranteed or fixed rate).

Step 3: What About Health Insurance?

For individuals evaluating early retirement opportunities, the provision of health care coverage to age 65 is a core concern. At 65, Medicare typically becomes one's primary source of health insurance. Supplemental coverage is often purchased to expand one's overall comprehensive health care plan. The period between early retirement and age 65 (when Medicare takes effect) is the variable.

Some questions to consider: Does the option exist to continue participating in your employer-provided insurance? If yes, at what premium rates? If no, have you explored your options in the individual health insurance market? Typically, a person should expect premiums to increase at the historical inflation rate. But a more conservative approach would be to plan for a 10% annual increase between your early retirement date and your eligibility date for Medicare. Visit www.healthcare.gov, your local insurance professional, or the Human Resources office at your work for more resources and information.

Step 4: Evaluating the Incentive

Many early retirement programs offer incentives for employees who accept them. Some questions you should be considering are: How might critical formulas that influence issues like eligibility to continue health care coverage be impacted? Are there enhancements to pay out of sick or vacation days?

If you were to compare these enhancements to what you save, invest, or accrue on an annual basis, how would these enhancements compare?

Step 5: Should You Keep Working?

To answer the question of whether or not you should just keep working, you should consider the following: What is the potential for my current position to remain viable beyond the early retirement program? And for how long? How transferable is my experience and skill set in the marketplace? To what extent am I willing to "re-tool" or "relocate" to continue working in today's economy? Do options exist for part-time work in my current or other positions between now and full retirement? While these questions are somewhat subjective and may be difficult to answer, they can serve as an additional filter or lens for your retirement evaluation process.

The all important evaluation of a retirement package is an enormous and complicated decision. While the steps outlined above are designed to give an outline of considerations, decisions of this magnitude may warrant the advice and perspective of a financial professional. A well trained financial professional will help with the objective aspects of the offer such as retirement income projections, debt elimination in retirement, expense summaries, health insurance considerations etc. But their counsel may go beyond these aspects and move into the subjective aspects of your decision as well. Decisions like these can be emotional and may benefit from the perspectives of an advisor who is not impacted by that part of the evaluation process. Remember, the cost of advice may be the fraction when compared with the potential expense of making a mistake at this crossroads of retirement.

Chapter 4

The Wellness Renegotiation

The Wellness Revolution

"As of 2012, about half of all the adults in the U.S. had one or more chronic health conditions, and one in four adults had two or more. The leading causes are tobacco use, poor nutrition, lack of physical activity, and excessive alcohol use. Even something as simple as getting people to follow their prescription drug protocol can be a difficult task. Recent surveys revealed that 50% of Americans diagnosed with a chronic condition do not take their prescribed medication after six months. Treatments cost approximately $2.9 trillion annually, which amounts to roughly 86% of the nation's health-related expense.

Consider a 55-year-old man with high blood pressure. Data shows that he can save more than $17,000 in cumulative preretirement out-of-pocket health expenses by following simple health management tactics, such as taking medications, limiting salt intake, and exercising. In retirement, this same individual would also be able to save an average of $910 in health costs each year. Individuals who suffer from conditions such as type 2 diabetes could also benefit from similar lifestyle changes."

—David H. Harris, V.P. Nationwide Retirement Institute

I am not a doctor, and I don't play one on television. I am not a health care practitioner, and nothing in this section is intended to be medical advice. Always consult your own health care professional before making changes to your own health, wellness, and vitality protocol.

The main point of this section is to summarize an issue that many of us already have experience with. We cannot continue to take poor care of our health and then expect "someone else" to pay for the treatment of our health conditions. We are the stewards of our own resources, including our health. Yes, there are times when an individual gets a sickness or disease through no fault of their own. There will always be factors outside of our control. Our goal here is to focus on our own personal responsibility. There is a potential multiplier in terms of vitality and quality of life. There is also a financial link. Some of the most important decisions we will ever make relative to our future financial condition begin with the responsibility we exert over our own health and wellness choices today.

Imagine an investment with a four to one return. You invest $1, and your "return" is $4. Would you make the investment? You are probably asking how long it might take to earn your $4 return or how much risk there might be along the way. These are great questions to explore. In this case, the investment is in your own health and wellness.

You have heard of the phrase "return on investment" or ROI. ROW refers to "return on wellness." Organizations that have begun adopting health and wellness programs for their employees have experienced substantial decreases in overall health care costs. Stress levels may be reduced, employee absenteeism declines, and overall health and productivity improve by as much as a $4 to $6 savings for each $1 invested in employee wellness. What if the same potential existed for the investments you and I could make into our own health and wellness? No financial professional is allowed to promise returns looking forward. But if we allow ourselves to consider this in terms of the context of potential savings in health care costs combined with enhanced quality of life, this investment merits our consideration.

This trend of investing in health and wellness is a positive innovation. Critics of the Western approach to health care state that we invest too much in solving health care problems and too little in preventing them. The approach of Eastern medicine is to focus more on health, vitality, and the prevention of disease.

When Benjamin Franklin stated that “An ounce of prevention is worth a pound of cure,” he might have been trying to direct the current health care industry!

“An ounce of prevention is worth a pound of cure.”
–Benjamin Franklin

Despite this “return on wellness,” there are those who may decide against a wellness program because “insurance doesn’t pay for it.” Obviously, it makes good sense to take advantage of benefits offered by your health care provider. But when someone decides against a treatment or path of wellness because it may not be covered by insurance, he or she has lost sight of the overall objective: to improve our own health, wellness, and quality of life.

We want to age well and thrive in each season of life. We also want to protect the assets we have accumulated over the course of our lifetimes. One of the best strategies to do so rests in the “negotiation” of accepting complete responsibility for our own health. This does not simply mean the absence of disease but also the presence of health and vitality.

"When health is absent... wealth becomes useless."
-Herophilus

As the cost of long-term care insurance skyrockets, fewer individuals can afford such protection. Medicare and Medicaid will both be strained by the 10,000 Baby Boomers turning 65 every day. Longevity is both a blessing and a challenge. Negotiating in this critical area of wellness is as simple as your next decision to begin an exercise or nutrition program or consult with a wellness professional. Your future may depend on it.

Our current healthcare system, as great as it is, has its limitations. For example, many individuals ask one primary question when considering a path to wellness or recommended course of treatment: "Is this covered by my insurance?" That question is understandable given the complexity and cost of our health care system. However, it can be short-sighted. That question also contains a premise that is somewhat misguided. The question assumes that there is "someone else" who pays for our health- care costs. Allow me to share an illustration that reveals who that "someone else" really is.

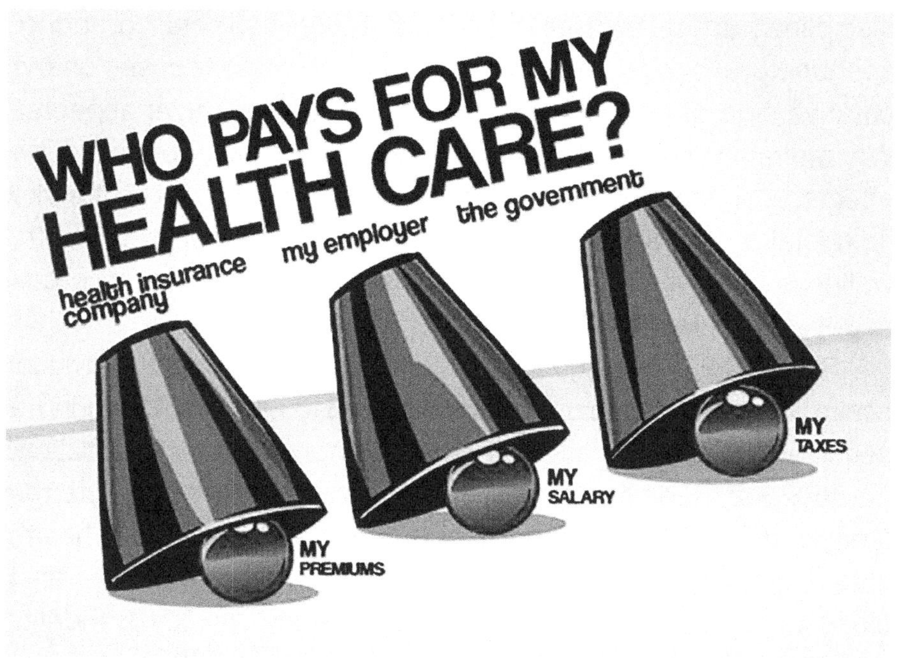

There are other questions we can ask at the same time as we negotiate the landscape of our own health, wellness, and vitality:

- What is the potential of this course of action to enhance my quality of life?
- Am I addressing a condition that may have minor consequences (i.e., an allergy) or significant issues (diabetes)?
- What are the potential expenses if I don't pursue the recommended path to wellness (potential surgical procedures, medications, treatments etc.)?

You and I are responsible for our own health. You and I are responsible for our own health. You and I are responsible for our own health. We may consult with physicians, nutritionists, chiropractors, personal trainers, etc. We may bring together disciplines from Eastern traditions (yoga, tai chi, qi gong, acupuncture) and Western medicine (which often focuses on the curative side of medicine rather than the preventative aspects). We make informed decisions about treatment options, side effects, and potential long-term impacts on our health. But make no mistake: You and I are solely responsible for our own health, wellness, and vitality. We are our own advocates. No one can negotiate this landscape for us.

Since 1999, average worker contributions toward individual health insurance premiums have risen 281% to $1,213 during a period of 47% inflation, according to the nonprofit Kaiser Foundation.

In 2002, Fidelity Investments conducted a study on the amount of funds a 65-year-old can anticipate needing for health care and out-of-pocket medical expenses in retirement. That study concluded that $160,000 was needed. In 2018, Fidelity updated that study. The updated amount ($280,000) represents a 75% increase! Your responsibility for funding your own health care needs in retirement will likely be your greatest single expense in this great season of life.

Introducing Your Future Health Care Advocate

This is an intensely personal story that brings home the sacred importance of being our own health care advocates:

> *We walked into the room with the team of health care professionals that had been pouring their hearts into Ginny's treatment. The months that had passed since her stroke were a reminder that much in our health care world arrives in shades of grey rather than black or white. She had been in and out of long-term care facilities, rehabilitation facilities, intensive care units, etc. Three steps forward... then two*

steps back. The hope of recovery with signs of progress adjacent to the sadness and discouragement of setbacks. Respirators, artificial feeding, antibiotics, heart rate monitors, and countless other machines and measures were all involved in the daily emotional ebb and flow of care.

Our family was emotionally exhausted from the ongoing care and coordination of care delivered by other health care professionals. Every decision was emotionally taxing. The truth is that we were probably making health care decisions from an emotionally compromised state. We would discuss options, choices, and next steps between our family, then make a decision. But as this meeting was about to unfold, there was a feeling of hollow acceptance as we sensed the choices in front of us. The doctors, nurses, and therapists each gave their assessment of Ginny's condition, the treatment she had been given, and their prognosis for her future. We had reached a point where she was no longer showing signs of potential improvement. In part, due to the miracle of modern health care, we were successfully keeping Ginny alive... even though there was no quality of life.

After the team shared their updates, my sister asked the question that we were afraid of but knew had to be asked anyway. She looked at the lead physician and asked, "What would you do if this was your Mom?" He looked at us with both compassion and conviction in his gentle voice: "It's time to let her go. We've done everything we can do for her. The stroke simply did too much damage."

There are five siblings in my family, and we knew we needed to have the private family meeting after the meeting with Mom's health care team. When one has fought at every turn to give someone every opportunity to improve, to recover, to heal, and the decision is made to give up the fight, the emotional consequences are almost traumatic. We cried our way through the family meeting and gave the medical team the okay to proceed. Breathing assistance would be stopped. Antibiotics would be discontinued. Artificial feeding would end. We discontinued the life-continuing treatments. At one point, when my sister was holding Ginny's hand as her frail body began to let go, she looked at me with tears in her eyes and asked, "Can you remind me why we decided this?" Second thoughts were on all of our minds.

After a moment to gather myself, I answered: "We didn't decide this. She did."

Several years earlier, Ginny had done the work of updating her legal and health care documents. First, she completed a health care power of attorney, giving a person she trusted the power to make decisions on her behalf when needed. There can't be a democracy when it comes to making health care decisions for someone. Completing this health care power of attorney gives one person the ability and responsibility to make timely, well-informed health care-related decisions if the patient is incapacitated. Ginny also prepared what are called advanced directives. In the event of a terminal illness, injury, or a situation from which one will not recover, these directives give instructions regarding the use of artificial feeding, antibiotics, respiration, and other life-sustaining measures. Putting these decisions into a written legal document gives guidance to health care professionals and family members so that your wishes will be carried out.

Ginny had suffered a major stroke. For stroke recovery victims, there are many shades of gray as one attempts to determine the difference between short-term damage from the stroke compared with long-term, potentially permanent damage. We had to navigate through the uncertainty of evaluating the short-term issues before the long-term/ permanent consequences became clear. Several days later, Ginny passed peacefully. The guidance she gave to family and health care professionals in advance provided a peace and reassurance that endure to this day. Her loved ones can rest, knowing that her wishes were respected.

The moral of the story is a simple one. *You* are your own health care advocate. Your wealth and your health are two life areas in which you must invest a lifetime of study backed with acceptance of responsibility. Of course, you are likely to partner with professionals in the care of your wealth and your health. But in the long term, they will need to be directed from your own compass of responsibility and guidance for the future in the event you are unable to make these choices for yourself. "An ounce of prevention" (in the form of advanced directives) is worth more than a "pound of cure." It is worth the peace of mind for yourself and anyone you entrust with decisions regarding your care.

Acknowledging that personal responsibility is
the only path to freedom
We make informed decisions
Taking action with the resources we have
Adjusting course along the way
Focusing only on what we can control
Until the future you envision in the present
Becomes the reality that you experience.

Chapter 5

The Stimulus Renegotiation

The Great Recession and The American Recovery and Reinvestment Act

Starting in the late 2000s and continuing through the early 2010s, The United States and other world markets experienced a general decline, the likes of which had not been seen for decades. While the timing and impact of the recession varied from country to country, this was considered to be the worst global recession since the 1930s and the Great Depression. Sadly, the Great Recession was caused largely by unsustainable lending practices in the United States' housing markets.

While the policies of other countries also played a part, the tendency of U.S. lenders to loan money to those who could ill afford it (through so-called "subprime" loans) resulted in a financial crisis that had ripple effects throughout much of the world. Ultimately, the financial crisis led to the collapse of banks around the world. As often is the case, the unintended consequences of one policy led to the crisis of the next policy. We wanted to make it easier for people to participate in the American dream of owning a home. We loosened lending standards. You may recall receiving ads in the mail for mortgages and home equity lines of credit based on 125% of your home's value! We created the bubble that ultimately burst into the financial crisis of 2008 (Source: http://economics.mit.edu/files/1801).

The U.S. response came in the form of the American Recovery and Reinvestment Act of 2009 (ARRA), also known simply as the Recovery Act. This was a dramatic stimulus package approved by Congress and signed by President Obama in February 2009. The ARRA's main purpose was ostensibly to preserve existing jobs and spur new job opportunities, to "jump start" the economy. Proponents also argued that the program would create temporary relief programs for people in need of help as a result of the recession and allow investment in education, infrastructure, health, and renewable energy.

When put into law, this stimulus package was expected to cost the U.S. $787 billion. Ultimately, it will cost at least $831 billion. As a result, the U.S. government's deficit spending (the amount of money the government spends versus how much it takes in) increased from $459 billion in 2008 to almost $1.5 trillion in 2009. In one year, our deficit spending more than *tripled*!

But why? Why did the powers that be choose to spend so much money? It all comes down to something called Keynesian economic theory. Named after John Maynard Keynes as a result of his 1936 book, *The General Theory of Employment, Interest and Money*, this theory holds that, in the midst of a recession, the government should try to compensate for a decrease in private spending by increasing public spending, the goal being to save or create jobs while stopping further economic declines. This theory was first developed during the Great Depression and put into place by President Franklin Roosevelt's New Deal, a series of stimulus and infrastructure programs.

So, that was the plan, to essentially spend our way to prosperity, to inject enough money into the economy that jobs would be preserved and created, banks would be shored up, and our roads and bridges would be improved as well.

Whether or not this actually helped is a matter of debate. Economists looking backward at the stimulus and subsequent unemployment rates are divided as to whether or not unemployment rates were improved as a result of the stimulus package.

But here is the kicker. The spending that ballooned starting in 2009 didn't stop there! Whereas 2008 deficit spending was $459 billion and the 2009 deficit spending was a whopping $1.48 trillion, deficit spending continued at much the same rate for the following years. We spent more than $1.3 trillion in 2010 and again in 2011 (Source: http://library.intellectualtakeout.org/library/chart-graph/federal-deficit-spending-billions).

FEDERAL BUDGET DEFICITS 1998 TO 2018

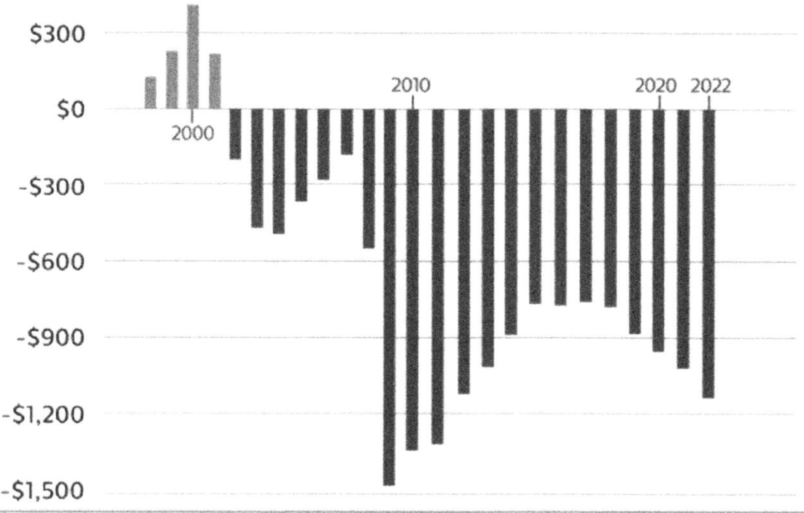

Sources: Office of Management and Budget, Budget of the U.S. Government, FY 2013: Historical Tables, Table 1.1, February 2012, http://whitehouse.gov/omb/budget/Historicals (accessed August 8, 2012), and Congressional Budget Office, An Update to the Budget and Economic Outlook: Fiscal Years 2012 to 2022, Alternative Fiscal Scenario, August 22, 2012, http://cbo.gov/publication/43543 (accessed August 23, 2012).

Recall the picture of the shell game that reveals that no matter who pays for health care, it ultimately falls under our responsibility. The same is true for government spending to stimulate the economy. When the government borrows money to stimulate the economy, that debt belongs to us. When interest rates are driven to near 0%, that impacts and penalizes those of us who save. And when inflation rears its ugly head (history indicates this is the inevitable consequence of printing money) once again, we end up footing the bill by paying higher prices for goods and services.

But why does this matter? What impact does it have on you?

Some of the answers to that question may not be known for many years. How exactly our government will address our long-term national debt is a subject for the ages... and one too complicated for this book. But there is a part of this equation that is impacting you right now. In fact, it has been affecting your savings (and, likely, your retirement) for years.

Quantitative Easing and Interest Rates

Part of the stimulus provided by our government was provided through what has been called "quantitative easing." This curious phrase is an invention of the last 20 years. It essentially describes the process of injecting money into an economy. Some would describe it as "printing money." The U.S. started employing quantitative easing in 2008, and this is the source of the deficit spending described above.

At the same time, interest rates were forced down to unprecedented levels. While interest rates have fluctuated throughout U.S. history, they dropped to their lowest point in the years during and following the Recovery Act of 2009. The government was willing to go to any means necessary to save and jumpstart our economy. It drove interest rates down to near 0%.

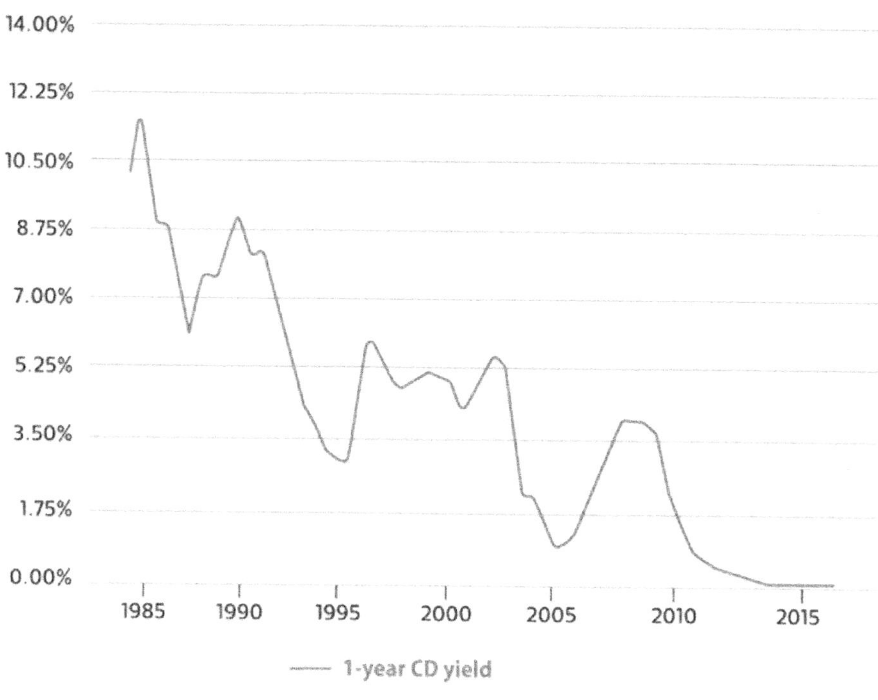

Source: Bankrate.com

You remember getting your bank statements where your earnings were essentially 0%. (As crazy as it sounds, some economies around the world had *negative* interest rates.) With interest rates near 0%, savers were effectively paying to guarantee someone else's principal. If you were a first-time home buyer, looking to purchase a new car, or wanting to make some other significant purchases, the presence of near 0% interest rates were a gift. Home mortgage rates were under 4%. In some cases, car loans were 0%! (Don't get me started on the cash for clunkers program and how much it cost!) Rates were lowered to encourage spending. The intention was to sell more cars and more homes and to spend our way to prosperity (or at least to recovery).

All of this was great if you were in the spending mode. But what about those who depended upon interest from savings for their living expenses?

When one part of an economy is stimulated, another part of the economy is punished. This is especially true when we discuss interest rates. If we lower interest rates to make it easier for people to *buy* things, we also lower interest rates for those people who lend them the money.

You may or may not be aware of this, but the money you deposit in a bank or invest in a CD does not simply sit in an account, waiting for you to withdraw it. Instead, that money is invested by the bank in several ways. Some of the money is lent to other members of the bank in the form of home or auto loans. Some of it is invested by the bank in other companies, commodities, etc. What the bank does not do with your money is let it sit idle. Idle money gets eaten up over time by inflation! So, instead, the bank uses your money to make the bank more money. This is one of the ways banks create profit for the bank's shareholders. The important part of this conversation for our discussion, though, is simply that your money funds the very loans that banks make to other customers. (Think back to the epic scene in *It's a Wonderful Life* where George Bailey, played by James Stewart, talks everyone off the ledge when they were making a run on the bank. This scene portrayed that the money the banks receive from one customer is then loaned out to other customers.)

To better illustrate the point, let's imagine that a bank takes your money and loans it directly to another customer to buy a home. To be competitive, the bank offers this mortgage (for the sake of our discussion) at a 4% interest rate. If the bank is going to earn 4% on the money it loans, how much interest can it afford to pay you for your money? Obviously, the answer is "less than 4%." How much less depends on many factors, but the takeaway is clear. If the bank is loaning money at a very low rate of interest, it can only stay in business if it pays out an even lower interest rate. This is why you saw the interest on your savings accounts plummet during and following the Great Recession and the corresponding Recovery Act.

Of Spenders and Savers

But it didn't stop with savings accounts. The CDs that formerly paid 6% now paid less than 1%. Annuities and many other yields dropped too. Sadly, these are the very same investments that many retired people counted on to provide them an income during their retired years. Many people on fixed incomes found themselves receiving less and less money.

And for those who lived off of their interest income, those funds did not experience the same type of recovery that impacted the stock market.

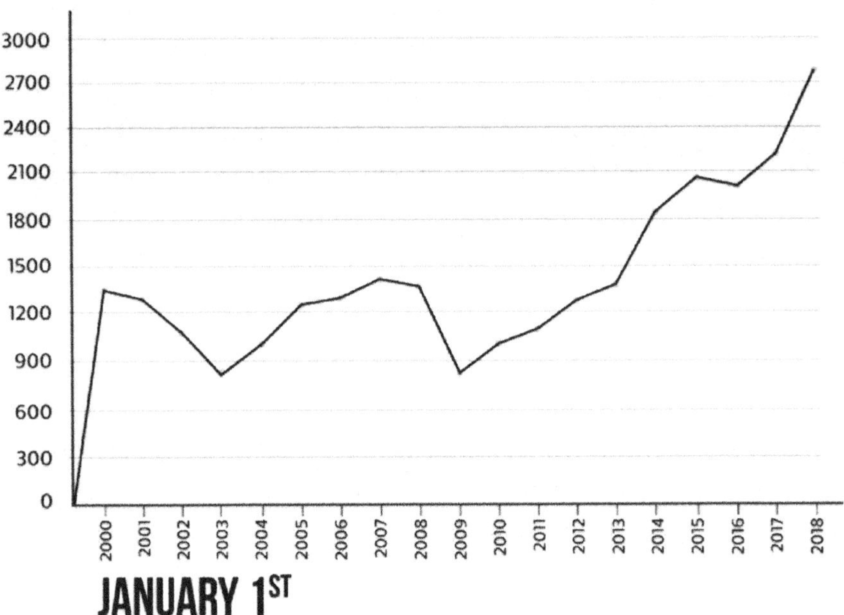

Sources: Standard & Poor's, Robert Shiller

Historically, the stock market recovers after periods of underperformance (it's never guaranteed, but it has been a pattern historically). Over time, people whose stock market investments fall during a drop in the markets will likely see their investment values recover. Even as devastating as the stock market correction was, the image of the market below shows that some markets had recovered to their previous levels in approximately five years. But many in retirement live on the interest generated from savings to cover living expenses. When a retiree's CD rate declines from 6% to 1%, the problem isn't simply that the income doesn't go nearly as far as it did previously. Many people in their retirement years choose to sacrifice the potential for growth to have investments that are perceived to be safe from market volatility. In other words, they choose more conservative investments and accept less upside to have less downside. When these conservative investments start to pay less, however, there is far less opportunity to replace these losses. While those fully invested in the markets might see their losses erased in a period of several years, those on fixed incomes or with more conservative investments might never see their losses fully erased.

The policy of economic stimulus as expressed in this country for the last 10 years has unfortunately punished savers and conservative investors. Savers have been punished in an effort to benefit spenders. This is a dangerous precedent with long-term implications. How will younger generations develop the habit of saving if they are not rewarded for it? Will a 20-year-old be inspired to put more money in savings after he sees his bank statement, where he earned $1.15 on a $10,000 savings balance? Or would he rather just spend his money on the latest iPhone? See the challenge?

In case you find yourself wondering how to protect yourself from government patterns and policies of stimulating spending and penalizing savings, consider the following possibilities (obviously in concert with a well-diversified investment plan):

- Insurance company annuity payouts may be based on longer-term periods than shorter-term vehicles like money markets and short-term CDs. As a result, they may offer a higher return.
- Stock dividends have historically been another way to generate income.
- Certain bonds are designed to be longer-term and may provide better yield opportunities than short-term instruments (but always beware of the fact that bonds have their own potential default and interest rate risk).

Remember the general guideline:

- When rates are below historical averages (at 5% to 6%), it may be a good time to lock in interest on debt (i.e., refinance your mortgage, car loan, etc.).
- When rates are above historical averages (at 5% to 6%), it may be a good time to lock in interest on savings (i.e., longer-term CDs).

Don't get caught up in trying to predict the top or bottom of an interest rate cycle. Not only is this not possible, it's unnecessary. Let historical averages be your guide, and make decisions based on the best information available at the time.

When the economy is fragile, the government tends to repeat its policies of stimulus. Be warned. In these situations, the rules of engagement favor the spender. One can always count on governments to act in their own best interest. These patterns, throughout history, rationalize the spending of long-term resources as an investment for a short-term recovery. Who pays? That would be you and me.

Acknowledging that personal responsibility is
the only path to freedom
We make informed decisions
Taking action with the resources we have
Adjusting course along the way
Focusing only on what we can control
Until the future you envision in the present
Becomes the reality that you experience.

Chapter 6

Renegotiation Resolutions

Your retirement has been renegotiated for you, whether you like it or not. But this does not mean you are helpless. In fact, there are a number of steps you can take to make your retirement the best it can be. One of the very first (and the most important) steps you can take is to educate yourself. As a reader of this book, you are to be congratulated. You are already far ahead of the average person. Frankly, you are a member of the elite, the very small percentage of people who go out of their way to learn more about finance, investing, and retirement. Your continued acquisition of knowledge in this area is probably the single most important factor for your future.

To help you along this road, here are several "resolutions" to aid you. These general principles and lessons will help you take control of your financial future.

The tools and strategies exist to start down a personal path of economic independence.

Resolution #1: The Accountability Negotiation (Never Accept Advice without Accountability)

They may be well-intended. They may honestly think they are helping you. They may even believe they could spare you from making a mistake. Who are the "they" that I am referring to? Friends, family members, coworkers, neighbors, workout partners, etc. are all a part of this well-intentioned group. They share financial tips with the testimonial power of an infomercial. They quietly filter out their mistakes while magnifying their victories. They quote "articles" they have read (often ads from social media or Google) and make you wonder how you have survived without their financial wisdom and discernment. They measure stock returns between arbitrary periods of time pretending to be Warren Buffett. They quote former game show hosts who now peddle products via infomercials and radio ads. They make it sound so simple. Yet you find yourself wondering if you're doing things the hard way… the wrong way.

I have a one word regarding these voices of financial chewing gum: IGNORE! STOP! RUN AWAY! Okay, that was more than one word. Do you get my point? First of all, these well-intentioned souls may really not know anything more about the financial world than you do. Second, their willingness to give "advice" should make you nervous all by itself. They generally have no professional licenses or certifications, have had no continuing education about the complexities of the financial world, understand little about long-term risk and reward, and have no accountability for the results of their financial guidance. Thank them for their time. Perhaps you can have a standard response, such as, "That's really interesting." Be warned that the information they share may not be accurate. If you were going to climb Mount Everest, would you watch an infomercial for a product for climbers, or would you hire a Sherpa who has successfully made the journey on a number of occasions?

Now, for the second group of people to steer clear of with regard to advice without accountability: the dreaded "experts." Maybe you have seen some of the compelling ads for...

The End of America 2010
The End of America 2011
The End of America 2012... Okay, you get the idea, right?

"Nobody can predict interest rates, the future of the economy, or the stock market. Dismiss all such forecast."

—Peter Lynch, Former Manager, Fidelity Magellan Fund

In today's world of media overwhelm, access to studio-quality video, and distribution lists, anyone can become an expert. All you have to do to become an expert is... well... call yourself an expert! If you make enough predictions, some of them will accidentally be right. An internet marketing "expert" begins touting the benefits of investing in Bitcoin from the stage. A larger-than-life (literally) personal development guru becomes an "expert" in money management. There is a fine line between entertainment and education. That line is frequently crossed. Let me pose a question. What do the following entertainers have in common?

- Tony Robbins
- Suze Orman
- Jim Cramer
- Dave Ramsey

There is not a single professional license, designation, or credential among them. The moment someone becomes licensed in the wealth management profession, they are subject to oversight by various regulatory bodies. The things that we do and say are all subject to regulatory and compliance oversight. This is the beginning of accountability. The next step of accountability is to engage in a long-term relationship with a client. The future of the relationship is dependent upon the quality and consistency of the advice provided along the way. This is often referred to as the "advisory model." There may not be a perfect model that ensures 100% success in reaching your financial goals. But we have the conviction that advice *with* accountability gives us the best opportunity to help you navigate the seasons and challenges of life.

P.S. One more word of caution: Be careful what you read.

The ultimate goal of any television or radio show is ratings. The goal of a program offering newsletters is subscriptions. The target for many financial publications is advertising revenue and distribution. Let's look at one example from a well-known magazine: *Kiplinger*. The topic involved here is one that has become an easy target for controversy: annuities.

The concept of an annuity goes back to the Roman Empire. Even in Latin, the term "annua" referred to annual stipends. The goal of this reference is not to begin an education on the many forms of annuities that exist today. With annuities, as with any other financial instrument, we believe they should be viewed from the lens of a simple question: "What problem does this help me solve?" The objective of this example is simply to illustrate the conflicting opinions that can even come from the same source (in this case, *Kiplinger*).

"When a financial advisor or insurance agent suggests you buy an annuity, is he looking to serve your best interests – or to collect an iPad and a trip to Aruba?"

Later in the same article....

> "...And investors should note that an advisor who discourages the sale of an annuity purchase may have his own conflict of interest."
>
> —*Kiplinger's* Retirement Report (January 2016)

In other words, your financial advisor may have a conflict of interest whether they do recommend an annuity or not! I am unsure how this contradictory narrative serves the overall goal of providing meaningful financial education. *Kiplinger* has historically taken a critical view of annuities until some insurance companies decided they were willing to buy them back. That's correct—insurance companies have been willing to pay clients to buy back the annuities that had previously been sold to them. In other words, the promises insurance companies made to the customer were more generous than the insurance company wanted to support. Even though these products have been criticized for being expensive and complicated, here is the *Kiplinger* author's words of wisdom to a client who is presented with an offer to sell their annuity back to the insurance company:

"Most seniors who own older annuities should spurn financial incentives to relinquish lucrative guaranteed income and death benefits" (Source: "Be Wary of Insurers Offering Annuity Buybacks," *Kiplinger*, January 2013).

Do you see the challenges inherent in taking financial "advice" from any source that is not accountable to you for the long-term outcome and impact on your financial strategy?

Resolution #2: The Conviction Negotiation

Here's Your Nobel Prize

In 2013, Eugene Fama won a Nobel Prize in Economics. Fama has invested decades into his research and observations that "markets are efficient." This phrase describes the concept that markets absorb information so quickly that it is generally impossible to outsmart or predict where the markets or securities are going to go next. (Don't tell this to Harry Dent, who has made a fortune over his career selling books and newsletters making more predictions than Nostradamus.) Fama's research helped popularize index or asset class based investing that seeks to capture the overall risk and returns of the market in general. There you have it. The Nobel Prize in Economics validates the efficiency of the markets. Unless it doesn't.

In 2013, Robert Shiller also won the Nobel Prize in Economics. Shiller's research brought him to a different conclusion than Fama. Shiller believes that his data indicates that in the long run, stock and bond prices can behave irrationally, reaching prices that are out of line with economic fundamentals. Shiller developed his own "Case Shiller Index" and predicted the dot-com crash of the early 2000s and the implosion of home prices in 2007. The Nobel Prize in Economics validates the observation that markets are not always efficient.

These are two completely contrary views of the markets and securities. There are two brilliant and accomplished academic minds behind each perspective. What conclusion should we draw from these contrary views? Perhaps one conclusion is that merely *having* clearly identified convictions is more important than *which* convictions one holds. Convictions are the lens through which we see our world and our finances. They keep us committed to our disciplines when markets are performing well and when they are not. In the absence of these convictions, a person may adopt one strategy during one season and subsequently adopt a different one during another season.

One discipline of investing is referred to as "buy and hold." This would fit under the umbrella of Eugene Fama's research. The underlying assumption is that history has indicated that the long-term trend is positive and that the declines have been temporary. Investments are held through the temporary setbacks to participate in the long-term advance.

Another discipline takes a more active approach to investment management. Sometimes, this is referred to as "active," "tactical," or "strategic" investment management. The goal of this more active strategy is to minimize the impact of declines while still participating in the positive trends.

ACTIVE MANAGEMENT VS. BUY AND HOLD

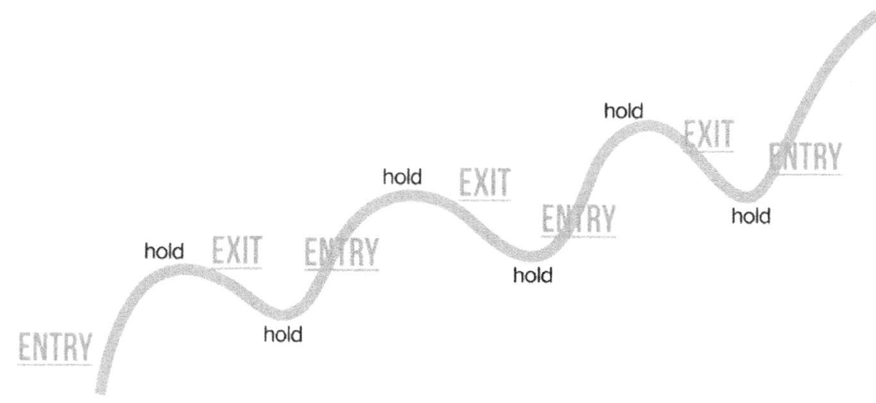

(For illustration purposes only. Not intended to predict a specific outcome or return.)

Which of these disciplines is correct? If you can tell me what the markets are going to do, I can tell you which discipline will work the best in any given season! Since we can't predict the future, we make informed decisions about strategy based upon the experience of the past and the convictions of the present. These convictions are essential, as they are the glue to stay committed to a strategy during the seasons when things don't go your way. In fact, it may be that a carefully coordinated approach that integrates both philosophies serves you well over time. While you may never win a Nobel Prize in Economics, your convictions may earn you a more important credential: a secure and prosperous retirement!

Investors Behaving Badly

Here is one additional perspective on the importance of having convictions as it relates to your investment strategy. Each year, a study is conducted that attempts to quantify the gap between investment returns and the returns investors actually earn. "Quantitative Analysis of Investor Behavior" is the long description of the annual study DALBAR conducts. When investments quote the returns that they earn, they will generally use a calendar period for measuring returns. The DALBAR study seeks to go an additional step. This study analyzes the patterns of individual investors and takes the specific timing of when they actually own a fund into account. Year after year, the study quantifies a major gap in investing. Consumers have a tendency to buy an investment after a period of positive performance and often sell that investment after a period of poor performance. In a sense, the gap is the difference between the performance of the *investment* and the performance of the *investor*.

In some cases, this gap may be caused by fear when markets or investments are in a downward cycle and an emotional decision to sell is made. Other times, the byproduct of "chasing returns" is when investments are purchased after a period of hot performance only to subsequently underperform. "Past performance is not meant to predict or guarantee future results" is more than a required disclaimer. It is also wise counsel. The same level of risk that can contribute to a cycle of outperformance can contribute to a potential correction or decline. The value of convictions is not grounded in the mythical/legendary quest to outperform the market. Convictions keep you grounded and focused throughout the changes and cycles that are the nature of the market. Consider the wisdom of Warren Buffett:

"We do not have, never have had, and never will have an opinion about where the stock market, interest rates, or business activity will be a year from now."

Average Investors Underperform Major Indices 1997-2017

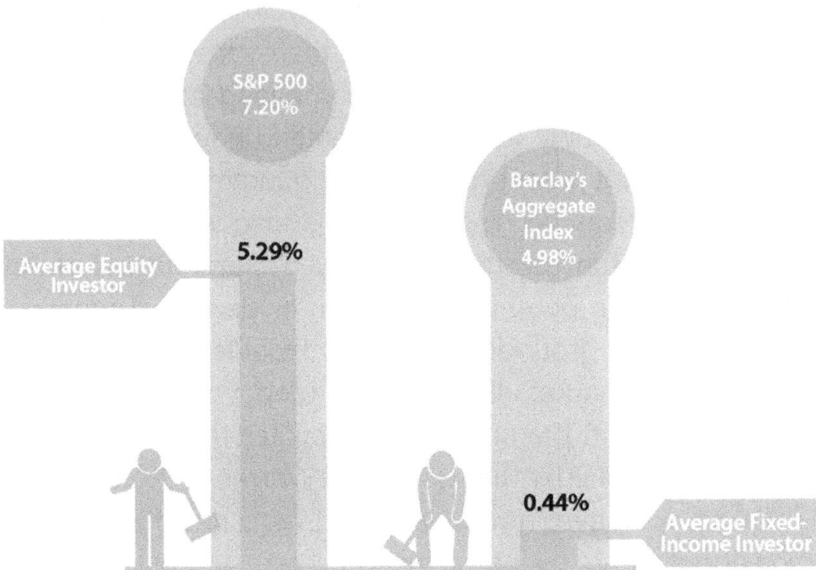

DISCLOSURE: Average equity and fixed-income investors returns calculated by DALBAR. DALBAR uses data from the Investment Company Institute (ICI), Standard & Poor's, Bloomberg Barclays Indices, and proprietary sources to compare mutual fund investor returns to an appropriate set of benchmarks. The study utilizes mutual fund sales, redemptions, and exchanges each month as the measure of investor behavior. These behaviors reflect the "average investor." Based on this behavior, the analysis calculates the "average investor return" for various periods. These results are then compared to the returns of respective indexes. Ending values for the indexes and hypothetical equity and fixed-income investor investments are based on average annual total returns. Standard & Poor's 500 Composite Index is a market capitalization-weighted index based on the results of 500 widely held common stocks. Bloomberg Barclays U.S. Aggregate Index represents the U.S. investment-grade fixed-rate bond market and consists of U.S. Treasury and government-related bonds, corporate securities, and asset-backed securities. Figures shown are past results and are not predictive of results in future periods. The market indexes are unmanaged and, therefore, have no expenses. Their results include reinvested distributions but do not reflect the effect of sales charges, commissions, account fees, expenses, or taxes. Investors should carefully consider investment objectives, risks, charges, and expenses. This and other important information is contained in the fund prospectuses and summary prospectuses, which can be obtained from a financial professional and should be read carefully before investing.

Reasons for the Gap

While we are on the topic of the importance of investor behavior, permit me to drill down on the vital importance of this topic. The reference to the DALBAR study above points to a behavior pattern that can contribute to poor investor returns on investment. Having watched this study for many years, the gap between the performance of the investment and the earnings of the investor tends to widen after bear markets (which, as of this writing, have not occurred in many years). Bear markets tend to magnify emotional decision-making. Especially for those who are close to or in retirement, watching values decline in the era of media inundation is emotional. A new discipline is developing called "behavioral finance," which is drilling down more deeply into the specific thought processes that lead to our decisions. Here are a few examples:

- Loss aversion: Nobel Prize winner Daniel Kahneman's research revealed that we are 2.25 times more driven by the desire to avoid loss than we are to achieve gain. Be aware of this in advance of the next market decline. Just because it is an emotional predisposition does not mean it needs to be acted on.
- Mental accounting: We have a tendency to compartmentalize buckets of money in varying and sometimes emotional ways. Money received from an inheritance might be viewed differently than money saved for retirement or as part of an overall investment plan. Money from an unexpected severance package may have its own mental construct. Be honest with yourself and your financial professional if you have different expectations or emotional attachments to your various buckets.
- Anchoring: Anchoring occurs when we get overly attached to a single piece of information. We may recall the all-time high for a stock that we own (when the stock

only knows what it is worth today on the open market). We may be reluctant to sell our home because we are fixated on what we paid for it, even if the purchase was during an inflated period for real estate. Stocks that are inherited are often associated with their price or value when a loved one passed away. Or we turn down a job that offers reasonable pay because we recall what we were making before The Great Recession.

- Familiarity bias: In today's environment of media overload and virtually unlimited options, people still have a tendency to stay in a narrow range of that with which they are most familiar. They listen to the same music and follow the same TV commentators even if it means they may be missing out on other important perspectives and options. In the world of investing, people may invest primarily in U.S. stocks because it is what they are most familiar with. In our increasingly global economy, this familiarity bias may mean missing out on opportunities around the globe.
- Gambler's fallacy: Suppose you are observing a quarter being tossed 10 times. Surprisingly, the first six times, the quarter lands with heads face up. The gambler's fallacy points to a belief that it is less likely to continue landing heads up because of the recent pattern. The reality is that every time a coin is flipped, it has a 50/50 chance of landing on heads or tails.
- Overconfidence: In 1999, more mutual funds earned over a 100% rate of return than any year in history. Who remembers? News magazines touted the "new economy" driven largely by tech stocks and pondered whether the markets would ever go down again. Investors poured into technology stocks in droves. We willingly suspended our understanding that wherever there is return, there is also risk. We all know what happened when that bubble burst!

- Herd behavior/social proof: We referenced the dot-com craze in the previous point. To demonstrate that we don't always learn from our mistakes, we followed a similar pattern with real estate leading up to the financial crisis of 2008. In the event you would like a more recent example of our tendency to follow the herd, consider the current cryptocurrency craze. The importance of a financial strategy is not merely in the areas upon which it will focus. Rather, its value can also be in protection from the areas of potential danger that can come from following the herd.

Source: Life Images

"People need to be reminded more often than they need to be instructed."
–Samuel Johnson

A Story of Trust

The "value" of a trusted guide in the increasingly complex financial world can also be expressed in human terms. I have had the privilege of speaking to and consulting with wealth management professionals from across the country. In fact, my second book, *Shaping the Future,* was the culmination of an extended period studying the beliefs and practices of some of the most successful wealth management professionals in the country. While delivering a keynote in Las Vegas to a group of advisors, I implored them not to take our clients' trust for granted. When we are immersed in the world of investment portfolios, financial plans, asset allocation, preparing clients for retirement, managing our offices, etc., it can occasionally distract us from the sacred trust that is behind every dollar that we manage for our clients. Yes, I believe it is a sacred trust. The Scriptures state in Luke 16:11 that "If you have not been trustworthy in handling worldly wealth, who will entrust you with true riches?" Therefore, the role advisors serve in the lives of our clients is also sacred. The message was extremely well-received, and I felt as though I had delivered the message I was given.

The next evening was a closing dinner. "Brett," a young advisor, approached me (he called me "Mr. Frank," which helped me realize the difference in our ages even more!). "Brett" asked if he could speak with me for a moment. My daughter, Nora, was with me and asked if I wanted privacy for the discussion, but "Brett" assured her she was welcome to stay.

"Do you remember," "Brett" asked, "that part in your talk yesterday when you pleaded with us not to take our clients' trust for granted?"

"I sure do," I replied.

"About that very time," he said, "I received a text message from the son of my largest client. The text message said, 'Dad just passed. We are going to be okay, right?'"

"Mr. Frank," "Brett" continued, "being able to reassure my client's son, to let him know he and his family would be looked out for, is priceless. Thank you for sharing the importance of our calling."

To this day, I marvel at the timing of this event. It was perhaps no coincidence that "Brett" received that text from his client's son just as I was speaking about this sacred calling. And I am humbled by the experience.

Resolution #3: The Incremental Negotiation

There are times when the reality check of planning for the new reality of retirement can seem overwhelming. Longevity, health care, inflation, underfunded entitlements, etc., can add up to factors that can make the creation of an adequate plan seem daunting. The incremental negotiation magnifies the long-term benefit of decisions that may seem small or insignificant at the time. Let's consider "The 1% Solution."

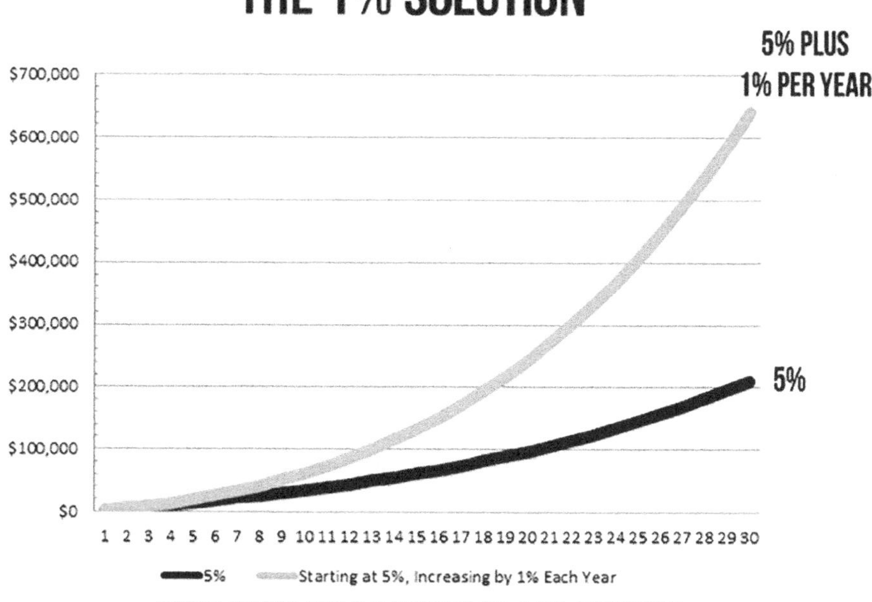

The 1% Solution

The following scenario is an example of just how much impact one percent can make: Two employees save 5% of their pay and earn a 6% return, with both earning $50,000 per year. Let's say the first employee keeps their contribution percentage level at 5% of pay, while the second employee increases the contribution percentage by 1% each year. After 30 years, the first employee has a balance of $210,320.34, and the second employee has *more than triple* that amount with $641,067.09.

Resolution #4: The Risk Negotiation

What happens when the greatest fear among retirees clashes with one of the primary risks in today's ever-growing season of retirement? In survey after survey, the number one fear cited by today's retirees is "outliving my money." People also fear losing money in the years just before or shortly after the start of retirement. These two issues can clash with the essential planning for longevity in retirement. If an individual says they can't afford to lose money in retirement, they are usually referring to the risk of decline in their investments. They may even quote the number of years it took the market to recover after the last downturn.

The alternative path is a strategy with little to no risk of downturn... and little to no risk of growth. Given the reality of a retirement season that may last multiple decades and health care inflation that can be substantially greater than the overall inflation rate, these understandable concerns may back retirees into a corner. In the desire to avoid "losing money," there exists the potential to lose "purchasing power" if safe and secure investments don't keep pace with inflation. Historically, investments that have provided safety fail to keep ahead of rising inflation. Even the increasingly popular "target date funds" (now the most widely utilized investment in employer-sponsored retirement plans) are designed to become increasingly more conservative as one nears their retirement or target date. Perhaps the following interaction helps illustrate the risk negotiation.

"What Kind of Risk Don't You Want to Take?"

Nancy called her financial advisor to make an additional investment to her account. She was already retired.

"I have some money I'd like to invest," she said, "but I don't want to take any risk."

There was silence for a moment. Then the advisor replied, "What kind of risk is it you don't want to take?"

"Pardon me?" she *said. "I don't understand. I said I don't want to take any risk."*

For most investors, "risk" means the risk of losing their money. More often than not, they are actually referring to the temporary decline in the value of their investments.

The question, "What kind of risk don't you want to take?" is an important one. Every investment and every decision comes with a certain amount of risk. Investing money in the stock market carries some risk that the value of the stocks may go down. Everyone knows this. To avoid risk, people may seek what they perceive to be less risky investments. Some people will place their money in a certificate of deposit (CD) at a bank because of a promise of a guaranteed return without the potential for a decline in value. What people often miss is the fact that even "safe" money is at risk in some fashion. Let's look at some cards I have created to illustrate this principle.

Many times, when I speak in front of groups of clients or potential clients, I use props. One of my favorite props to use is a set of five 24" x 36" cards. They look like giant poker cards. On one side of each card is a benefit; on the other side, however, is the risk associated with this benefit. For example, the "jack" in my deck shows an investment that is safe from current taxes is typically at increased risk for future taxes. The "king" shows that an investment that has a high potential for growth also has a higher risk of volatility.

These concepts have been so well-received by clients that I had my project manager create a desk set for both of my office locations too! Now, when a client like Nancy says she wants to invest her money in a way that is safe from something, like market swings, for example, I can hand her the "ace." When she flips it over, she sees that this so-called safety from market swings means her money is at greater risk from inflation.

Whenever I am discussing risk with clients, I ask the same question: "What kind of risk don't you want to take?" This serves as a reminder that there is no such thing as a risk-free investment. There is only the informed acceptance of risk on the path to accomplishing your retirement goals.

As a financial advisor, many of my communications are so unnecessarily complex that they can be bewildering. So, in order to communicate in the clearest and most concise manner, I am sharing this tool with you. It is my goal to find ways to reduce complexity, and ultimately increase your knowledge and understanding in a unique and engaging manner.

Here are the cards:

Safe from the Government:

Many investors want to make their investments safe from any risks associated with the government. To protect their money, they invest in items they think are out of the reach of the government. They invest in precious metals, purchase other currencies, or otherwise move their money "offshore," investing in companies or funds that are unlikely to be vulnerable to confiscation (or taxation) by the U.S. government. While these measures may make these investments "safe" from the authorities, these investments are at increased risk of other calamities.

Political changes in the world can rapidly change the value of these investments. Currency fluctuations (or collapse) can dramatically affect the value and security of money invested abroad. And the precious metals markets cans change quickly as well. While these investments are so-called "safe" from the U.S. government, the truth is that they are at risk from the actions of other governments. As you can see, avoiding one risk can expose you to many other risks.

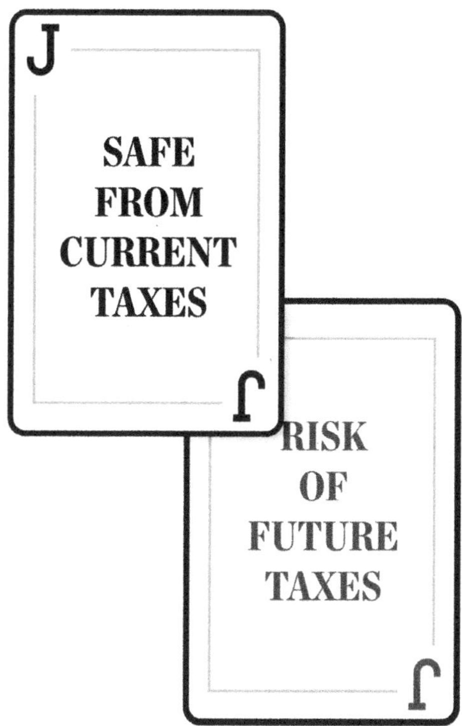

Safe from Current Taxes:

In our current tax environment, people understandably want to limit what they pay to Uncle Sam. I think we all want to keep as much of what we earn as possible. As such, investors often want to minimize their taxes, seeking investments that are tax-free or tax-deferred. Placing money in a 401K or other tax-deferred vehicle can be an important strategy to save for retirement.

First, you need to know that very few investments are truly "tax-free." The government goes out of its way to make sure it can collect taxes on every possible dollar. Second, tax-deferred investments are just that: investments for which taxes are *deferred*, not avoided. While current taxes can be avoided, taxes must ultimately be paid on that money.

For this reason, money that is safe from current taxes is at risk of future taxes.

Cash on Hand:

Some people wish to avoid the (unlikely) risk of temporary bank closures or the chance that they won't be able to get their hands on their money when they really need it. Natural disasters and extended power blackouts can render money saved in a bank account out of reach for days or even weeks at a time. As a result, some people squirrel money away, either in a safe or drawer at home, taking precautions for a rainy day when they will need the money. Some people save cash. Others buy and save gold bullion or silver coins. Still others save gems or jewelry.

This behavior is not limited to elderly spendthrifts stuffing their mattresses with cash or doomsday "preppers" socking away resources in case of a zombie apocalypse. Many people make efforts to keep a certain amount of cash and other resources on hand just in case they need it. These can be very useful measures to take.

But people need to understand that this money is not safe. While it may be safe from the potential closing of banks or an extended power blackout, it is vulnerable to other risks. A flood or fire can destroy or scatter this money. Thieves can break in and steal it. Disgruntled (or dishonest) family members may take it. Sadly, all of these things happen. Furthermore, insurance coverage for home caches of cash, precious metals, and jewelry may be limited. In addition, cash saved at home is at risk of ever-present inflation, becoming worth less and less each month. This is just another example where money that is safe from one risk is exposed to other risks.

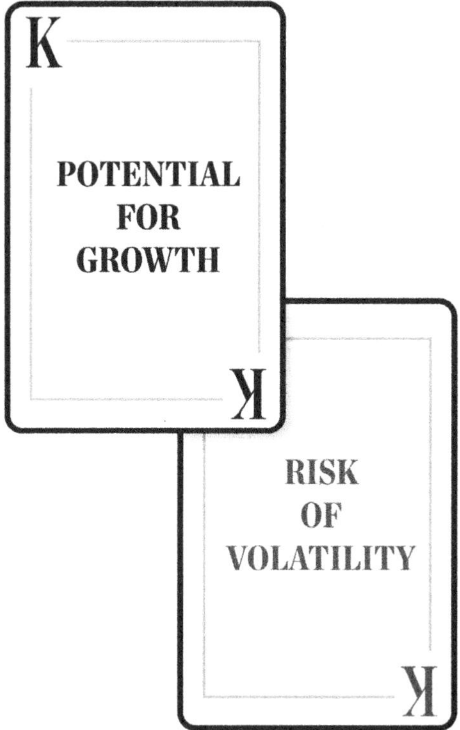

Potential for Growth:

Most people make investments to see the value of these investments increase over time. Very few people invest with the hope of losing money! The potential for growth is the often the most powerful incentive for investment. As such, investors seek opportunities to grow their investments over time.

With the opportunity for growth, however, comes the risk of volatility. Markets that move up also move down. While this volatility allows investments to grow, it also allows them to shrink. Money invested in the markets through individual stocks, mutual funds, and other vehicles share this inherent risk. Particularly as people approach or begin retirement, they increasingly desire to insulate their investments from the possibility of a market crash or drop. As a result, there are many different investment options that attempt to shield investors from this risk of volatility, limiting exposure to drops in the market. These investments, while safer from market fluctuations, also have a more limited opportunity for growth. The potential for growth and the risk of volatility are two sides of the same card. You cannot have one without the other.

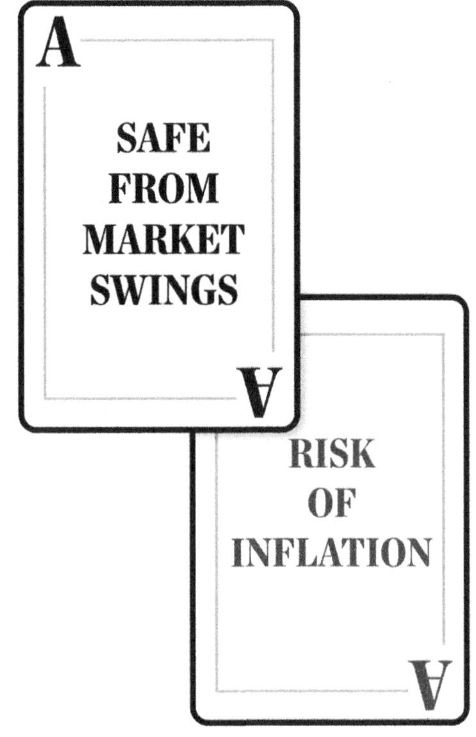

Safe from Market Swings:

Frankly, many people cannot tolerate watching their investments move up and down. Some experience severe anxiety when they think about the possibility that their retirement accounts may drop significantly due to a swing in the stock market. These people desire an investment option that is safe from market swings.

If you want to make your money safe from the volatility of the markets, you have many options. You can place your money in a checking account, buy certificates of deposit (CDs) from a financial institution, or otherwise take your money "out of the market." You can invest in any number of investment products that completely eliminate the chance that your money will go down if there is a stock market crash or correction.

But everything comes with some kind of risk. Remember? In this case, money that is safe from swings in the markets is at risk of being eaten away slowly by inflation. Although the rate of inflation is relatively low (right around 2%) at present, it hasn't always been this way. Inflation was at 18% in 1946. At the end of the 70s, we saw 13% inflation. Investments that are safe from market swings usually have lower (but perhaps guaranteed) returns when compared to more volatile investments. These lower (but "safer") returns are at risk of being eaten up by inflation, especially when inflation rises (Source: https://www.thebalance.com/u-s-inflation-rate-history-by-year-and-forecast-3306093).

No Risk-Free Investment

As you can see, there is no such thing as a risk-free investment. Every type of investment (whether made through an advisor, a bank, or through the lid of your piggy bank at home) has inherent risks. Every benefit has a risk associated with it. Savings kept at home are at risk of theft and fire. Money invested abroad may be "safe" from the government but at risk of problems from political turmoil and currency fluctuations. Investments made to avoid taxes today will be at risk of taxes in the future. Money kept safe from the changes in the markets may sacrifice potential for growth and be whittled away by inflation.

That being said, there are strategies to help mitigate risk. In fact, one of the best ways an advisor can serve you is to help you understand your risks and the potential for reward and to develop a strategy for your future. Because of their comprehensive knowledge of the types of investments available, they are uniquely equipped to help you navigate the risk/reward proposition.

Resolution #5: The Debt Negotiation

"Americans aged 60 to 69 had about 2 trillion in debt in 2017, an 11% increase per capita from 2004, according to New York Federal Reserve date adjusted for inflation. They had $168 billion in outstanding car loans in 2017, 25% more per capita than in 2004. They had more than 6 times as much student-loan debt in 2017 than they did in 2004, Federal data shows" (Source: "A Generation of Americans Is Entering Old Age the Least Prepared in Decades" by Gillers, Tergesen and Scism, June 22, 2018).

As we map out our strategy for retirement, the following question often arises: "Do I focus on adding to my investments or paying down debt?" As always, the specific answer varies based on your unique circumstances. However, here are some general guidelines for this kind of decision-making:

- Never leave an employer match on the table.

If your employer has a matching contribution on your retirement plan, make it a priority to earn the maximum match.

For example, let's assume your employer will match $0.50 for each $1 you contribute up to 6% of your retirement plan. Failing to earn the maximum matching contribution is like leaving a pay raise on the bargaining table! You just contributed 6% into your retirement plan, and with the magic of the employer-matching contribution, 9% went into your account (not to mention the tax deduction that was generated for your contributions as well).

- The closer one gets to retirement, the greater the emphasis should be on eliminating debt and associated payments.

Remember Einstein's quote that "Compound interest is the eighth wonder of the world"? Compound interest can only work its magic if given the important element of time. The importance of establishing wealth-building habits at a young age cannot be overstated. But what happens as we approach retirement and find ourselves having to play catch-up? Perhaps there is more benefit in eliminating payments than there is in adding additional funds to retirement accounts. Freedom from car payments allows every limited dollar of retirement income to stretch even further. Freedom from a mortgage payment in retirement eliminates the largest payment that is in most people's budgets. By some budget calculators, the typical mortgage payment can be up to one-third of a household budget. There are certain financial decisions that can be discerned when analyzing them from a cash flow perspective.

Let's say one has a current mortgage balance of $150,000, a monthly mortgage payment of $1,000 and aims to retire in 10 years. They have $500 a month to either add to their mortgage payments or save for retirement. If that $500 per month is invested for 10 years with an average earning of 6%, one will have saved $79,085, generating $263.55 per month in retirement based on a 4% withdrawal rate. However, if that $500 per month goes towards mortgage payments instead, one could pay off their mortgage by their retirement and save themselves $1,000 a month in retirement!

The other benefit to eliminating debt goes far beyond a financial statement. There is a peace of mind factor to consider. Individuals who have successfully eliminated their debt have peace of mind, emotional calm, and freedom to make different financial decisions than those who carry debt into retirement. We are learning more and more all the time about the impact stress can have on our physical bodies. Retirement is intended to be a season when you are free to focus on your life's purpose, live out your legacy, and enjoy the fruits of your labor. Freedom from debt can be a catalyst to your financial and emotional well-being.

Resolution #6: The Time Negotiation

There are many "sins" as it relates to the successful achievement of the retirement you envision. The fear and overwhelm of the 24-hour news cycle are enough to scare almost anyone into poor decision-making. The nature of our consumer-driven economy is like a daily conspiracy encouraging spending over saving. The adjustable rate or interest-only mortgage was the avenue to owning your dream home... until the dream became a nightmare when the payments went up and up and up (or your income went down due to corporate downsizing). The six months/same as cash purchase looked innocent at the time of the purchase. But the retroactive interest charges were like corporal punishment for instant gratification. According to Dave Ramsey's Financial Peace University, 75% of individuals who make these purchases do not pay off the item during the interest-free period. The timeshare that looked like such a smart way to vacation ended up being a cash flow drain you didn't anticipate.

We have all made mistakes when it comes to financial decisions. But there is one mistake that exacts a toll that can be more substantial than others. In fact, some refer to it as "the unpardonable sin" of wealth management. Welcome to your biggest enemy: procrastination. Many of the financial mistakes we all make prove to be potentially valuable learning experiences. But procrastinators incur a cost they can never recover... time. For compound interest to truly be the eighth wonder of the world, as Einstein put it, time needs to be our ally. To the procrastinator, time becomes the enemy. To the "negotiator," time can be a powerful multiplier. The power of the following case study should not be lost because of the frequency with which it has been shared:

Let's say we have two hypothetical lenders named Amy and Ben. Amy invests $2,000 per year beginning at age 30 and then stops investing after 10 years, with a $20,000 total contribution. Although she is no longer contributing to the account, she leaves her money in the account to grow for an additional 25 years. Ben doesn't start investing until age 40, contributing $2,000 per year for a total of 25 years (up until the day he retires) with a total contribution of $50,000. Amy invested $30,000 less than Ben, but gave her money 10 more years to grow, and ended up with a much higher account balance at retirement.

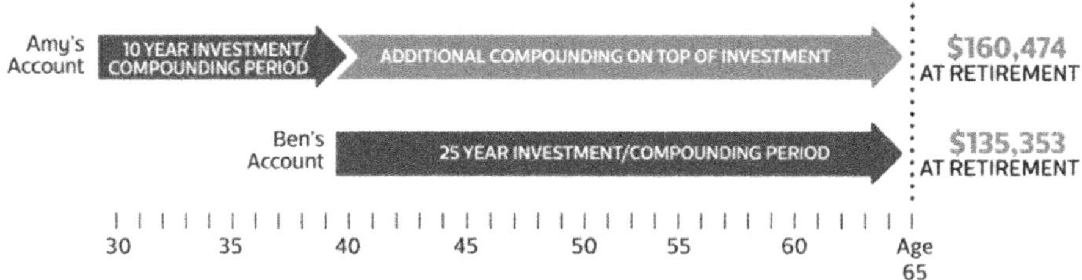

Resolution #7: The Sequence of Returns Negotiation

You've done all the right things. Your plan takes everything into account from longevity to health care. Your plan takes inflation into account and projects a rising income pattern so that you maintain your purchasing power throughout the upcoming season. A thoughtful analysis of your Social Security options has helped you land on the option that fits in with the rest of your plan. You have turned in your notice to your employer and gone through the customary retirement parties... and then, reality sets in.

There is one major factor that was left out of your equation. This factor has been referred to as "sequence-of-returns risk." This risk is best understood in the form of a question: "What if the stock market goes into a significant decline in your early years of retirement?" The bear markets of 9/11 (the dot-com bubble bursting and the 9/11 tragedy) and the financial crisis of 2008 led to an overall market decline of nearly 50% (as measured by the broad market indexes). If another such downturn occurs in your early years of retirement, how will your plan survive? The following chart helps illustrate the potential impact of this sequence-of-returns risk and the importance of having a strategy to address it.

DAVE AND JOAN

Sequence of returns: Poor, then strong

JEFF AND WENDY

Sequence of returns: Strong, then poor

Dave and Joan: Hypothetical Net Return	Withdrawal	Balance	AGE	Jeff and Wendy: Hypothetical Net Return	Withdrawal	Balance
		$500,000	65			$500,000
-27.1%	$25,000	346,275	66	26.7%	$25,000	601,825
-16.5%	25,750	267,638	67	10.1%	25,750	634,259
-1.9%	26,523	236,535	68	4.3%	26,523	633,869
3.1%	27,318	215,702	69	8.9%	27,318	660,534
10.9%	28,138	208,009	70	17.6%	28,138	743,697
-9.4%	28,982	162,199	71	22.5%	28,982	875,527
7.4%	29,851	142,141	72	-3.7%	29,851	814,385
8.1%	30,747	120,417	73	18.1%	30,747	925,477
15.4%	31,669	102,415	74	-6.1%	31,669	839,286
9.4%	32,619	76,356	75	9.2%	32,619	880,880
6.2%	33,598	45,410	76	7.6%	33,598	911,675
12.4%	34,606	12,143	77	9.6%	34,606	961,268
2.8%	12,143	0	78	22.4%	35,644	1,132,964
11.4%	0	0	79	-11.0%	36,713	975,663
9.0%	0	0	80	24.3%	37,815	1,165,745
24.3%	0	0	81	9.0%	38,949	1,228,207
-11.0%	0	0	82	11.4%	40,118	1,323,532
22.4%	0	0	83	2.8%	41,321	1,318,113
9.6%	0	0	84	12.4%	42,561	1,433,720
7.6%	0	0	85	6.2%	43,838	1,476,055
9.2%	0	0	86	9.4%	45,153	1,565,407
-6.1%	0	0	87	15.4%	46,507	1,752,811
18.1%	0	0	88	8.1%	47,903	1,843,006
-3.7%	0	0	89	7.4%	49,340	1,926,397
22.5%	0	0	90	-9.4%	50,820	1,699,273
17.6%	0	0	91	10.9%	52,344	1,826,444
8.9%	0	0	92	3.1%	53,915	1,827,478
4.3%	0	0	93	-1.9%	55,532	1,738,278
10.1%	0	0	94	-16.5%	57,198	1,403,702
26.7%	0	0	95	-27.1%	58,914	980,350
Average Annual Net Return		6%		Average Annual Net Return		6%

*The returns shown above are purely hypothetical and are assumed to be net of all fees and expenses. The balances shown above are end-of-year and reflect an assumed annual withdrawal of $25,000 (increasing 3% annually for inflation) taken at the beginning of the year. The above illustration does not illustrate any particular type of investment.

Source: Securian Financial Group

To illustrate how sequence-of-returns risk works, we'll take the above as a hypothetical example of two different couples who are just entering retirement: Jeff and Wendy and Dave and Joan. Now, let's reverse the rate-of-return sequence for each couple's investment to illustrate the impact. Both couples begin with a portfolio balance of $500,000 and make 5% annual withdrawals ($25,000 plus annual increases to account for inflation) over 30 years. Both couples expect the same average annual net return of 6%. Dave and Joan experience poor early returns and strong returns later on, which results in a depleted investment portfolio by year 13 at their mutual age of 78. On the other hand, Jeff and Wendy experience positive returns in the early years, and negative later on, still leaving them with a comfortable portfolio at their mutual age 78 and well beyond.

There are multiple strategies available for dealing with sequence-of-returns risk. One strategy is often referred to as the "bucket approach." In this framework, assets are invested in different buckets that correspond to their intended purposes. The long-term bucket may have investments with greater growth potential to combat inflation. The short-term bucket may have very safe investments designed to provide any necessary anticipated withdrawals, perhaps over the coming five-year period of time. Another approach is to use insured solutions to provide income that may be insulated from market volatility. The specific strategy you use is perhaps less important than the fact that you have a strategy for dealing with this type of risk. Your failure to anticipate and plan for this type of risk can lead to consequences that became all too common after the last two epic market declines: retirees headed back to work!

Resolution #8: The Market Negotiation (Be Careful What You Ask For)

"Why don't my investments grow as fast as 'the market?'"

In times when markets are trending higher, investors have a tendency to believe that wealth management is a sprint, and they don't want to miss out. However, the perspective that an advisor may bring is the reminder that retirement is more of an endurance race than a sprint. The following chart can highlight the contrast. One chart shows the S&P 500 and its value over time. The second chart illustrates the very different outcome that may result when market fluctuations are combined with withdrawals to provide retirement income during the same period. When we re-evaluate from the context of considering withdrawals in the new reality of retirement, we are reminded that each leg of a race must be evaluated in light of the fact that we are not in a sprint. Your endurance race known as retirement must guide these essential decisions.

GROWTH OF $1 JAN. 1927 - DEC. 2017

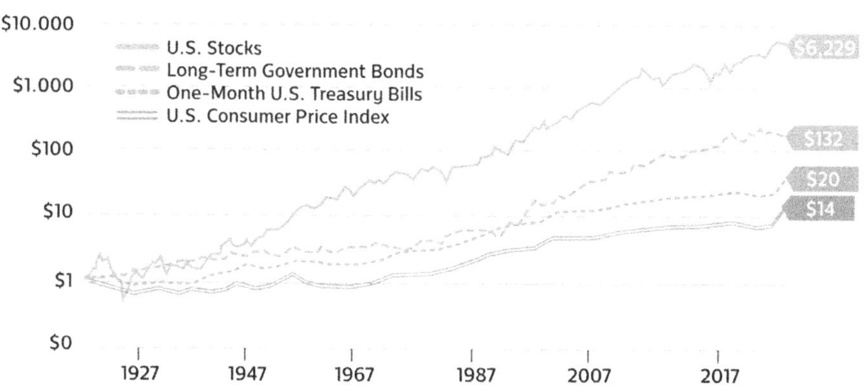

Source: DFA Returns 2.0. Hypothetical value of $1 invested at the beginning of 1927 and kept invested through December 31, 2017. Assumes reinvestment of income and no transaction costs or taxes. This is for illustrative purposes only and not indicative of any investment.

HOW WITHDRAWALS IMPACT A PORTFOLIO

Impact of a 5% Withdrawal

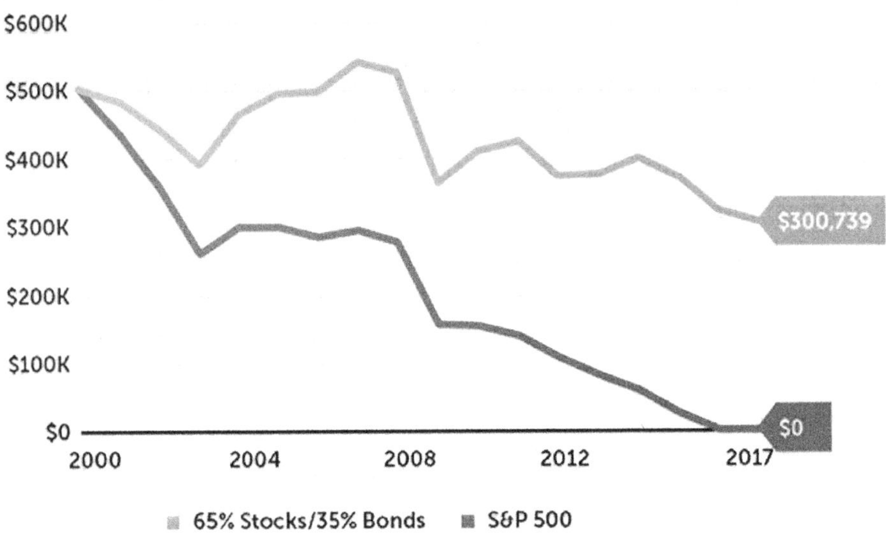

Source: Morningstar Direct 2018. Hypothetical value of $500,000 invested on January 1, 2000, and kept invested through December 31, 2017. Withdrawal is 5 percent of initial hypothetical value ($25,000 of initial $500,000 starting value) taken out at the start of each year, growing by 3% per year.

The S&P 500 Index (Standard & Poor's 500 Index) is an unmanaged market value-weighted index of 500 stocks that are traded on the NYSE, AMEX and NASDAQ. The weightings make each company's influence on the index performance directly proportional to that company's market value. Investors cannot invest directly in an index. Indexes are unmanaged and reflect reinvested dividends and/or distributions, but do not reflect sales charges, commissions, expenses or taxes.

Resolution #9: The "Bullseye" Negotiation

Elder abuse has become a multi-billion dollar industry. It is estimated that over $2.9 billion is lost per year due to financial fraud. Why is there a bullseye on your back? Because you have money. The mere fact that you have achieved a station in life where you have financial resources also makes you a target for abuse/fraud. Sadly, many individuals who are victims of financial fraud do not report it due to embarrassment or guilt. Social media, phishing schemes, and opportunistic and unscrupulous financial firms are all contributing factors to this multi-billion dollar problem. Perhaps the most disturbing statistic is that nearly 25% of elder abuse is caused by family members! Financial opportunities that sound too good to be true, investment or lending opportunities that prey upon the good intentions of others, medical breakthroughs in anti-aging drugs and supplements, "lottery" winnings, and the compounded access to information that is the internet all make for ripe pickings for those unscrupulous predators. Sadly, family members who make an appeal to the emotions of retirees are the icing on the cake of corruption. As we age, we tend to experience diminished mental sharpness or acuity, which means we must take even more care to safeguard our life savings. Here are a few common-sense measures we can take to safeguard a life's worth of hard work:

- Adopt a 24-hour rule.

No financial decisions should be made under pressure. Whether the pressure is a "limited time only" pitch via phone or delivered online, give yourself a safeguard against making any decisions under pressure. This will allow you the time to do some research to determine if the opportunity is legitimate. It may also give you time to take advantage of my next suggestion.

- Form a "digital neighborhood watch group."

A neighborhood watch group is an agreement among neighbors in a community to all keep an eye out for each other's properties. If we see anything suspicious, we report it. We have each other's backs (or back yards!). A digital neighborhood watch group extends this idea to cybercrime. If you receive an email with an offer that sounds too good to be true, news about a breakthrough medicine only available through specific outlets, high-pressure limited time offers, or investment opportunities that seemingly defy every limitation of risk and return, you connect with your digital neighborhood watch group and ask if anyone has had any experience with the product or service being offered. Those who are concerned can also check in with Consumer Reports, AARP, and other watchdog groups.

- Monitor your financial accounts regularly.

There are a variety of tools available that can help you monitor your financial accounts on a regular basis. Even though a number of these tools are "free," be careful. In general terms, "free" to the subscriber means subscriber data is sold to firms that market financial products and services to you. Generally, platforms offered by wealth management professionals and firms have higher security and appropriate policies regarding the safeguarding of your data. Start the process with firms where you have an existing financial relationship (bank, brokerage firm, financial advisor), and always ask about their policy regarding sharing data with other firms. Some cutting-edge systems will trigger an alert to the client and advisor in the event of unusual activity in the various financial accounts. Early detection is essential for damage control if your data is compromised.

- Engage a trusted voice outside of your family.

Given that an estimated 25% of elder fraud cases are caused by family members, there can be merit in having an objective source of guidance or feedback without the emotional attachment of family. Whether this is a trusted friend or a financial professional, the benefits of objectivity are significant. Emotions can cloud judgment. A decision to "help" a family member may be well-intentioned but can lead to both greater family and financial stress.

- Beware of the "free dinner" where the same product or service is right for everyone.

Several years ago, a colleague related the following story:

A prospective client came into my office with a stack of paperwork that looked like it weighed two pounds. She was in her 50s at the time.

"I need you to tell me this was a good idea," she said as she moved the paperwork to my side of the table. "My mom went to a free dinner and said she really liked this guy. This is what he did with her money."

Before I began reviewing the documents, my instincts told me there might be trouble. By the time I was done reviewing the paperwork, it was clear that over 80% of her mom's money had been put into an investment that was not liquid and would not be for some time (10 years, in fact). I asked a few questions to better understand what the goals were for these funds. She explained that this was conservative money that needed to be accessible in the event her mom needed it for health care-related expenses. While there was a narrow provision that provided greater liquidity in the event of confinement to a nursing home, this was not a liquid investment. As I backtracked with the client, she said that her mom kept telling her, "This man [hosting the free dinner seminar] seemed so genuine and sincere." Her options to access her funds over this 10-year time period were now very limited. In short, aside from pursuing some legal or regulatory remediation, there was little that could be done.

Good, bad, or otherwise, a common way for those selling financial investments to meet new prospective clients is to host a free dinner. This can be a very effective way for an advisor to meet new potential clients and begin a relationship that can be valuable for both parties. In and of itself, there is nothing wrong with this.

The problem comes when everyone in attendance gets the same recommendations from the speaker. It's like magic! Even though the people in attendance have varying needs and backgrounds, everyone gets the same pitch. Very often, what is pitched is some magic legal instrument that eliminates taxes, bypasses probate, reduces complexity in your estate, and guarantees harmony among your beneficiaries for generations! Or, it's the unicorn of investing products, a product that promises you can 1) receive all the gains when the markets goes up, 2) experience zero losses when the markets go down, 3) access your funds in the event of an emergency, and 4) pay zero fees.

First, much like unicorns, such an investment simply does not exist. Second, every investment has a fee factored in somewhere. Any person who ever tells you an investment product has no fees is being less than honest with you. And if they are willing to lie about fees, they are likely to lie about other things too!

This situation is not a judgment on evening, educational, or even free-meal events. These can be a legitimate path to get to know a professional and their offerings. Just keep in mind that it would be highly unusual for the exact same financial product or solution to be a perfect fit for everyone in the room.

As a result, here are some questions you should always ask:

- What problem of mine does this solve?
- How does this apply to my specific circumstances?

Just remember this: Use your common-sense filter whenever a single product or strategy is recommended for every person in the room, especially when it has no apparent downsides, risks, or expenses. Every strategy and every investment vehicle has its upside potential, risks, and its tradeoffs or limitations. Understanding all aspects is vital to effective decision-making.

Resolutions Summary:

Keep these resolutions in mind whenever making financial decisions. These can help you avoid a great deal of heartache and help you in your journey to and through retirement. While not all of these will apply to you right now, the odds are great that this advice will pay off for you down the road. Above all, continue to employ your own common sense, but also seek and conscientiously follow wise advice.

Where there is no guidance, a people falls,
but in an abundance of counselors there is safety.

—Proverbs 11:14

Conclusion

Acknowledging that personal responsibility is
  the only path to freedom
We make informed decisions
Taking action with the resources we have
Adjusting course along the way
Focusing only on what we can control
Until the future you envision in the present
Becomes the reality that you experience.

You won't see this notion on the evening news. You won't find it on covers of bestselling books. And it is not attractive enough for the so-called "market experts" and their endless newsletters, audio programs, seminars, and trading systems all claiming to have the secret sauce to financial independence. Even though this concept gets little notoriety, it is the first key to your future in retirement.

Personal responsibility is the only path to freedom.

There you have it. Shall I repeat it again?

PERSONAL RESPONSIBILITY IS THE ONLY PATH TO FREEDOM.

Some of the changes to this landscape may seem completely outside of our control. Government stimuli, advances in health care and longevity, and the continued underfunding of entitlement programs are all factors outside of our control. However, the strategy we employ to navigate and negotiate these factors is completely *within* our control. We are responsible for our own choices and, ultimately, our financial well-being. Tomorrow will largely be influenced by the choices you make today. As a mentor of mine once said: “Some people make excuses. Other people make progress. You get to choose.”

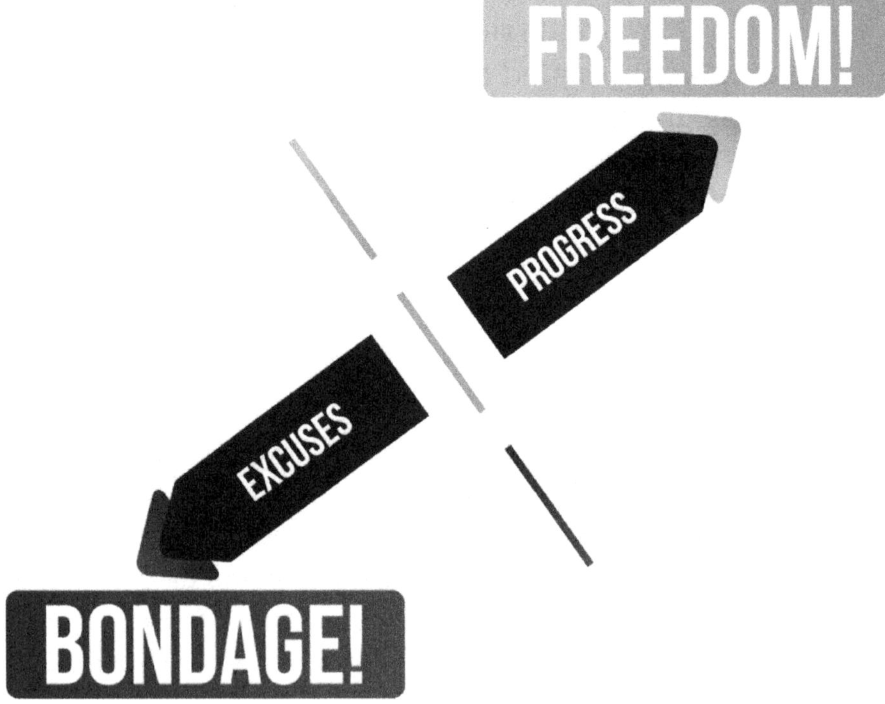

We need to take this premise of personal responsibility one step further. Some of us need to clean up the messes of our past before we can seriously begin to shape our futures. One cannot “negotiate” with a future that is rapidly unfolding without coming to grips with the consequences of past decisions. According to

Dan Sullivan, "All progress begins with the truth." If your truth is one of a present state of bondage because of previous decisions of indebtedness, let's address that truth.

If you have made poor financial decisions in the past, admit the truth and forgive yourself. Allow these mistakes to turn into lessons, and move ahead on a path toward financial success. There are times when an individual may berate themselves (or their spouse) for some poor financial decisions. Will you give me permission to share a distinction that you may find empowering? Guilt is a feeling we experience when we look back with regret to a decision that has been made. It is only empowering if it leads to the sister emotion of conviction. Whereas guilt looks backward with regret, conviction looks *forward* with determination. It is a decision with resolve not to repeat mistakes from the past. Forgive where you have been, admit where you are, and decide to move forward. We must negotiate this internal challenge before we can navigate the external ones.

With the guilt of the past converted into a *conviction* to guide us into the future, let's address the factors that are under our control. Using some of the techniques discussed in Chapter 6, you can begin to take control of your future wherever possible:

- Employ the **1% Solution** to systematize your saving. Consistently saving and then increasing that saving will help bring true financial health.
- **Reduce debt.** Even if you can only make inroads a little at a time, start now. Remember, "The borrower is servant to the lender" (Proverbs 22:7).
- Put your knowledge of the **Risk Negotiation** to work for you, acknowledging that, sometimes, the avoidance of one type of risk will expose you to other risks. Know your risks and mitigate them when possible.

- Employ the **24-Hour Rule** to avoid high-pressure or impulse purchases.
- Establish and participate in a **Digital Neighborhood Watch Group.** Be on the lookout for suspicious emails or offers, and share your findings with others.
- **Monitor your financial accounts** regularly.

Now, let's return our focus to some of the external negotiations that can only be made from a place of strength:

- **Avoid generic or one-size-fits-all financial solutions.** You are an individual with unique values and needs. As such, any solution designed to work for everyone is not designed to work for you!
- **Never accept advice without accountability.** Avoid the so-called "gurus" who dole out financial advice without oversight and without consequence for poor counsel.
- **Engage a trusted voice outside of your family.** Find a qualified, independent, and accountable source for financial guidance. A well-qualified advisor can guide you through *all* of the negotiations covered in this book.

A select group of wealth management professionals are grounded in preparing for these realities and serving clients who are willing to travel the path of personal responsibility. Samuel Johnson said, "people need to be reminded more often than they need to be instructed." If you are curious about the potential value of a voice that consistently reminds and instructs, consider the Russell Investments 2017 study on the value of a financial advisor. It was found that, on average, "advisors are worth up to four times the 1% fee" generally charged for managed assets. The study considered the different ways financial advisors deliver value, including the annual re-balancing of investment portfolios, preventing behavioral mistakes that individual investors often make, the cost of basic investment-only management, planning costs, ancillary services, and tax-aware planning and investing. It was concluded that "the single largest contributor to the total value advisors bring is being a 'behavior coach' to their clients." While most advisors would never make the claim that their services are worth an extra 4% return per year, the Russell research points to the benefits of a trusted advisor. Even if you consider your financial knowledge to be above average, people still need reminding more often than they need instruction. And sometimes, that value is beyond measure.

Although successful stewardship is based partly on knowledge, it is also based heavily on behavior. Your retirement has been renegotiated for you... and not to your benefit. Increasing longevity, government spending, artificially suppressed interest rates, underfunded pensions, and rising health care costs have delivered a costly blow to the retirement you had hoped to plan. The good news is that you do not have to be a passive victim to these factors. In fact, you shouldn't be! You now have the power to renegotiate your retirement again; only this time, it will be in your favor. With the expanded awareness you have gained from this book, the wise counsel of a financial advisor, an acceptance of personal responsibility, and commitment to action, you are equipped with the tools and strategies necessary to head down a personal path of economic independence. You *can* reclaim your future.

Remember, time is the enemy of the procrastinator and the ally of the negotiator. Let's put the time remaining to work for you!

The future has several names.
For the weak, it is impossible.
For the fainthearted, it is unknown.
For the thoughtful and valiant...
It is ideal.
–Victor Hugo

About the Author

Frank A. Leyes, ChFC® is a nationally recognized speaker and the author of the Amazon bestselling book, *The Way of Wealth*: 7 Steps to Financial Freedom in a World of Economic Dependence.* A highly successful financial professional with over three decades of experience, Frank manages practices in Indianapolis, Indiana and Roanoke, Virginia and speaks and consults with other advisors around the country all while prioritizing time with his family at their home in the Blue Ridge Mountains. Frank uses his gifts of speaking, writing, and counseling to help individuals and advisors create futures forged through the path of personal responsibility.

Frank A. Leyes, ChFC® can be reached at:
http://www.frankleyes.com/

---

* The Way of Wealth, Amazon, 8/27/13, #1 in Money Management and Retirement Planning. Amazon Best Seller rankings were calculated hourly based on number of copies sold on 8/27/13 in a chosen subcategory compared to similar books in the same subcategory. Subcategories were self-selected and some subcategories contained more books than others. Recent sales were weighted more heavily than past sales. A ranking within a subcategory is not representative of total sales or placement within Amazon's overall sales list.

Made in the USA
Columbia, SC
15 October 2022

69298396R00068